Ag Bun na Cruaiche

Ag Bun na Cruaiche

Folklore and Folklife from the Foot of Croagh Patrick

Caitríona Hastings

Nonsuch

I dedicate this work to the memory of the pupils and teachers who collected these traditions, and to the many interviewees who shared their memories with them during the Schools' Folklore Scheme, 1937-8.

Go gcúití Dia a saothar leo uilig.

First published 2009

Nonsuch Publishing
119 Lower Baggot Street
Dublin 2
Ireland
www.nonsuchireland.com

© Caitríona Hastings, 2009

The right of Caitríona Hastings to be identified as the Author
of this work has been asserted in accordance with the
Copyrights, Designs and Patents Act 1988.

This publication has received support from the Heritage Council
under the 2009 Publications Grant Scheme.

British Library Cataloguing in Publication Data.
A catalogue record for this book is available from the British Library.

ISBN 978 1 84588 943 2

Typesetting and origination by Nonsuch Publishing
Printed and bound in the UK by Athenaeum Press Ltd., Gateshead, Tyne & Wear

Contents

Buíochas

Gabhaim buíochas le gach duine a chuidigh liom agus mé i mbun oibre ar an tsaothar seo. Is mian liom foireann Leabharlann Mhaigh Eo agus foireann Ionad Oidhreachta Chuan Modh a lua, as ucht a ndíograise agus a gcineáltais i gcónaí. Buíochas le Brónach Joyce agus Aiden Clarke as a gcuid tacaíochta, agus a gcuid eolais a roinn siad liom go fial. Bhí Emer Ní Cheallaigh, iarchartlannaí Roinn Bhéaloideas Éireann thar a bheith cabhrach i gcónaí agus gabhaim buíochas léise chomh maith. Buíochas le Harry Hughes a thug cead dom úsáid a bhaint as íomhánna óna bhailiúchán féin de sheanphictiúir agus cártaí poist agus le Caitríona Bn. Uí Raghallaigh a cheadaigh dom pictiúir as an leabhar *Schooldays in the Shadow of Croagh Patrick* a úsáid. Buíochas speisialta le Aiden Clarke a ghlac cuid mhór pictiúr de na scoileanna agus de nithe eile nach iad, agus le Liamy McNally a sholáthair pictiúir eile dom. Chabhraigh Críostóir Mac Cárthaigh agus Jonny Dillon liom agus mé sa tóir ar phictiúir i Lárionad Uí Dhuilearga in Ollscoil na hÉireann, Baile Átha Cliath agus tá mé an-bhuíoch do Chríostóir as roinnt pictiúr a chur ar fáil agam le húsáid anseo. Rinne Ivor Hamrock amhlaidh freisin nuair a chabraigh sé liom seanchártaí poist a fháil as an chartlann atá ag Leabharlann Mhaigh Eo. B'iontach an taca í Yvonne McDermott agus mé ag streacháilt le cúrsaí teicneolaíochta agus tá mé fíorbhuíoch di. Agus mé ag lorg eolais ar thraidisiún na n-amhrán sa cheantar, fuair mé cúnamh nach beag ó Úna Bean Uí Choinn ar saineolaí í sna cúrsaí sin. Óna cuid taighde féin a thug sí an t-eolas dom ar 'Slán le Muirrisc' agus gabhaim buíochas ó chroí léi.

Is é an tOllamh Séamas Ó Catháin, Stiúrthóir Lárionad Uí Dhuilearga do Bhéaloideas na hÉireann agus Cnuasach Bhéaloideas Éireann a thug cead dom na téacsanna béaloidis a chur i gcló anseo. Gabhaim buíochas leis. Is leis an Lárionad cóipcheart an bhunábhair seo uilig.

Ar deireadh, mo bhuíochas le m'fhear céile Gary as a chomhairle agus a chuid tacaíochta i gcónaí.

This material is published by kind permission of the Director of the National Folklore Collection, School of Irish, Celtic Studies, Irish Folklore and Linguistics, University College Dublin.

Introduction

The past is a foreign country, they do things differently there.

L.P. Hartley

This book presents folklore and folklife traditions collected in and around Westport, Co. Mayo, in 1937-38, under a scheme known as the Schools' Collection. Folklore, or 'béaloideas' in Irish, has been explained as that part of our culture which is passed on orally, aurally and by imitation. In Irish we use the term 'ó ghlúin go glúin', literally from knee to knee, to describe the natural process through which traditional knowledge of every kind has been transmitted down the generations. The terms 'memory culture' and 'unofficial culture' have also been used to indicate the nature of folklore.

In recent times the wider term 'Intangible Heritage' has been coined. In 2003, UNESCO, adopting the Convention for the Safeguarding of Intangible Cultural Heritage, defined this material as:

> The practices, representations, expression, as well as the knowledge and skills, that communities, groups, and, in some cases, individuals recognize as part of their culture. It is sometimes called living cultural heritage, and is manifest *inter alia* in the following domains:
>
> Oral traditions and expressions including language;
> Performing arts;
> Social practices, rituals and festive events;
> Knowledge and practices concerning nature and the universe; traditional craftsmanship.[1]

UNESCO's broad understanding of Intangible Heritage perfectly matches the scope of the material assembled under the Schools' Collection in the 1930s. Importantly, it was neither anthropologists nor sociologists who assembled the collection, but the young children of the area. On the eve of the Second World War, the children of the National Schools in the Republic of Ireland were organised to collect and document their own particular and unique local culture. It is a valuable resource for us now.

'A MEMORY BANK...'

In a millennium lecture, the poet Seamus Heaney referred to cultural heritage as 'a dream bank, a memory bank'.[2] Heaney warned that the humanist heritage of Europe was in danger 'of being slighted in favour of a new technological culture'. While the new culture could speed up the exchange of information, it could 'never quite establish a perspective upon it'. He added that cultural heritage provides a viewfinder for the individual self. I believe the folklore preserved in the Schools' Collection, and presented here, fulfills those same important functions outlined by Heaney. It affords preserved local information, but more than that, it gives perspective on the material. It provides the reader with a viewfinder with which to see the present. It is an important archive of memory, and now it seems that enough time has elapsed to render it of interest and value to us. After seventy years, we can have perspective on this era of the past. Socio-economic conditions have improved so much in the interim that it is now easier to look back with interest to those other days when life was more difficult here in the West. The collection illuminates every aspect of that time, but it also sheds light on our own time by giving us a local point of reference from which to evaluate the changes that have taken place.

THE SCHOOLS' SCHEME

The senior pupils in nine national schools in the parish of Aughavale, under the direction and guidance of the principal teachers, undertook the collection and recording of the folk traditions. Not all the primary schools in the parish participated in the survey, which was known officially as The Schools' (Folklore) Scheme (Scéim na Scol). The schools that participated were: Brackloon N.S.; Bouris N.S.; Christian Brothers' Boys School, Westport; Kilsallagh N.S.; St Patrick's N.S., Lecanvey; Murrisk N.S.; Teevenacroaghy N.S.; St Columbkille's N.S. (The Quay School), and the Convent of Mercy N.S., Westport.

The Schools' Scheme was devised by Séamus Ó Duilearga and Seán Ó Súilleabháin of the Irish Folklore Commission.[3] It was carried out in co-operation with the Department of Education and the Irish National Teachers' Organisation. Using a handbook[4] provided by the Folklore Commission, and under the weekly guidance of their teachers, the national school children collected the folklore, mainly from their parents and grandparents and other older members of the local community.

ARCHIVE

As a result of the Schools' Scheme we have more than 500,000 manuscript pages of folklore preserved in the archives of the Irish Folklore Commission, now held in the Department of Irish Folklore at University College Dublin (recently renamed UCD Delargy Centre for Irish Folklore and the National Folklore Collection).[5] A significant part of the material is bound and paginated in 1,128 volumes. The rest of it is contained in a large collection of the school copybooks into which the raw material was originally written by the children. The folklore that was collected in each county may also be accessed on microfilm in the respective County Libraries. The material from 292 schools in Mayo is available under licence in the Local Studies Department of Mayo County Library, Castlebar.[6]

COLLECTING

In the foreword to the handbook, *Irish Folklore and Tradition*, the senior pupils were:

> …invited to participate in the task of rescuing from oblivion the traditions which, in spite
> of the vicissitudes of the historic Irish nation, have, century in, century out, been preserved
> with loving care by their ancestors. The task is an urgent one for in our own time most of
> this important natural oral heritage will have passed away for ever.

The urgent note sounded here is familiar to the folklorist; things are always about to change dramatically it seems. Now, with hindsight, we can see that this ambitious project did take place at a crucial time, as the world geared up for the Second World War. After the war many things would have changed, here in Ireland as well as in the rest of Europe. The Schools' Scheme, which spanned the years 1937 and 1938, could hardly have been planned at a better time.

SCOPE OF THE SURVEY

In thirty-seven pages of the handbook the Commission outlined the areas of tradition which were considered worthy of investigation. They gave a range of questions under each topic, to guide the young collectors. It is useful to show here the topics suggested in the booklet, as the collected material corresponds to these categories. If the children collected a good deal of information on

'Hidden Treasure' in their localities, it is as a result of that topic being highlighted in the handbook, as much as anything else. Here is a list of the topics to be investigated:

> Hidden treasure; A funny story; A collection of riddles; Weather lore; Local heroes; Local happenings; Severe weather; Old schools; Old crafts; Local marriage customs; In Penal times; Local place names; Bird lore; Local cures; Home-made toys; The lore of certain days; Travelling folk; Fairy forts; Local poets; Famine times; Games I play; The local roads; My home district; Our holy wells; Herbs; The potato crop; Proverbs; Festivals; The care of our farm animals; Churning; The care of the feet; The local forge; Clothes made locally; The local patron saint; The local fairs; The landlord; Food in olden times; Hurling and football matches; An old story; Old Irish tales; A song; Local monuments; Bread; Buying and selling; Old houses; Stories of Giants and Warriors; The Leipreachan or Mermaid; Local ruins; Religious stories; The old graveyards; A collection of prayers; Emblems and objects of value; Historical tradition; Strange animals.

Instead of their usual weekly composition, pupils in fifth and sixth class (eleven to fourteen years old) were given time to write down in their copy books the folklore which they had collected that week. Much of that material was then copied into a logbook, either by the teacher or by the pupils themselves. In this collection, entries from two schools, CBS Westport and Convent of Mercy Lecanvey, were almost entirely written into the log by the respective principal teachers, based on the information collected by the pupils. In the case of the other schools, the entries are either handwritten by the children themselves, or, if written by the teacher, attributed to the child from whose book they are copied. The material presented here is based on the microfilm which represents the text in the logbooks from each school.

LANGUAGE

The bulk of this corpus of oral tradition is recorded in the English language, which was certainly the first language of the majority of people in this area in the 1930s. As early as 1908 the linguistic trend towards English had been noted:

> Irish is seldom used in Westport except by the people who come in from Mount Partry district. Most of the people who live in the vicinity of the town, as well as a large portion of the townspeople, know Irish, but they have got into the habit of not using it. They are now teaching Irish in the monastery and convent schools, and are generally girding up their loins, and preparing to rout the giant of Anglicisation...

The linguistic trend noted here by A. O'Gorman in *The Leader* of 25 July 1908 would continue, as Irish gave way to English. Despite O'Gorman's best wishes, there was little that the schools could do to change the trend.

THE HUNGRY THIRTIES — EMIGRATION

This Schools' Collection took place before the advent of rural electrification, which arrived in the late 1940s. Ireland would soon be in the grip of 'The Emergency' (as the war period was referred to). The level of poverty was very high in many areas of rural Ireland in the 'Hungry Thirties'. Many people were still earning their livelihood on the land, where most farms were small holdings. But the economic war of the 1930s began the shift away from the land, as farmers were unable to earn a living wage from their work. Emigration was an escape route for many. An article published in *Mayo News*, 13 February 1937, describes the depressed economic circumstances of the time. The article is titled 'Emigration to England', and the writer states:

> It is estimated that up to 40,000 young boys and girls left Ireland for England in search of work last year (1936). The exodus still continues and on last Friday contingents left different railway stations in Mayo for Cross-Channel destinations. Several people left Westport on Friday, and according to information received from rural areas, hundreds of young men and girls are eager to get away, there being no work for them at home…

The tragic consequences of emigration were felt deeply in the area when, on the 16 September 1937, ten young Achill harvesters lost their lives in a dreadful disaster when their bothies were burned down in Kirkintilloch, Scotland. The bodies were carried by train from Westport to Achill on the last leg of the terrible journey home.

At the beginning of January 1938, the Society of St Vincent de Paul in Scotland issued a letter underlining the dangers of emigrating to Scotland without due preparation and the certainty of employment. People were finding themselves destitute and dependant on relief, having tramped long distances in search of work.[7] Still the exodus continued. On 18 June 1938, *Mayo News* carried a further report, 'hundreds of emigrants left Westport Railway Station for England and Scotland. Fleets of buses conveyed harvesters from Achill Island to Westport.'

SOCIAL CONDITIONS AT HOME

Attempts were being made to provide employment at home. The late 1930s and early 1940s saw the growth of factories in Westport. Irish Sewing, Westport Doubling and the Reliable Shoe Company were set up. By the mid-1940s these businesses provided over 400 jobs for the town and the outlying areas. These jobs were sorely needed. On 8 October 1938, *Mayo News* carried an account of hundreds of 'refugees' returning from their employment in Britain, fearing the threatened war. One young man returning to Westport from London had a gas mask with him. Asked why he left London, the man said that when he saw Hyde Park being dug up he thought it time to get out.

Social conditions were slow to change in rural Ireland. The plague of tuberculosis only began to be combated in the 1940s. There was a pattern of late marriages and the birth rate was very high. Living conditions were very basic in most homes; it was unusual for people to have access to running water or sanitation. There were very few modern conveniences. Married women seldom worked outside the home and children would have worked on the family farm as required.

School attendance for children between the ages of six and fourteen became compulsory in 1926. The subjects studied included Irish, English, History, Arithmetic, Geography and Music. Girls also received instruction in needlework. Only a small number of pupils proceeded to secondary school.

As for social life, people provided their own pastimes and amusements. They told stories, sang songs, played music and danced in their homes. They visited their neighbours regularly for conversation and recreation. In the 1930s few people would have owned a radio. On 20 March 1937, *Mayo News* reported that it was estimated there were only 2,260 wireless sets in Mayo, i.e. one for every seventy people in the county. Transport was limited. A new Hopper Bicycle was advertised in *Mayo News* in April 1937 at a cost of £4 15s. A Cycling Club was formed in the same month.

Most entertainments were homemade, though the cinema was a very popular attraction in those days. In February 1937 'a very interesting film of Knock Shrine ... was shown to an appreciative audience in the New Cinema, Westport'.[8] In January 1938, The New Cinema Theatre in the town was showing a range of films; *White Fang, Half Angel, A Day at the Races* and *One in a Million*.[9] The Lecture Hall on the Newport Road in Westport was used for dances, concerts, boxing tournaments, badminton, socials and as a venue for travelling shows.[10] On 13 August 1938, the *Mayo News* reported on the growing interest in dance halls, 'Despite the heat of the weather during the past fortnight, dance halls in Westport district were crowded out for every dance and all records were

Westport Station.

broken in Lecanvey on Thursday night when nearly 400 dancers from all over the county patronised a dance at this popular resort.' In the same year, St Patrick's Musical Society performed a production of *Mikado* in Westport Town Hall.[11] Team sports such as Gaelic football and soccer were also important pastimes and there was keen rivalry between the parishes and townlands. Fairs, patterns and festival days punctuated the whole year, providing opportunities for wider social contact. They were keenly anticipated.

THE BEGINNING OF CHANGE

This collection of folklore comes largely from the pre-technological, pre-industrial era. Change had come gradually up until this point. By the time the Second World War was over, many of the old ways would be swept away, and most importantly perhaps, a new mentality would prevail. Although it might take some time to acquire all the trappings of modernity, the trend was established and the desire was there. The folklore collected by the pupils indicates the beginnings of that change in various aspects of people's lives. In recording the oral tradition of their own communities in this way, at such a pivotal time, they have left us a valuable legacy – an insight into the cultural heritage of this place before modernisation and globalisation. These children, born in the 1920s, would become adults in a much different world to their parents and grandparents.

EDITING

The collected material reproduced in this book is a selection of the material held on Reel 43 of the Schools' Collection in Mayo County Library, Castlebar. This reel contains a microfilmed copy of the manuscript pages that are bound in two volumes in the Schools' Collection in the UCD Delargy Centre for Irish Folklore and the National Folklore Collection: NFC.137 – pp 138-277, and NFC.138 – pp 1-554. The material is collated as follows:

St Columbkille's N.S., Westport Quay, S137, pp 138-231.
Convent of Mercy Girls' School, Westport, S137, pp 232-277.
St Patrick's N.S., Lecanvey, S138, pp 1-140.
Christian Brothers' N.S., Westport, S138, pp 141-199.
Bouris N.S., S138, pp 200-227.
Kilsallagh N.S., S138, pp 228-276.
Teevenacroaghy N.S., S138, pp 277-340.
Brackloon N.S., S138, pp 341-514.
Murrisk N.S., S138, pp 515-554.

The handwritten material from each school was transcribed in its entirety and then each item was classified under sub-headings in the eight chapters presented here. Very few spelling or grammatical changes were made to the material as they were not necessary. Material in the Irish language is accompanied by my own literal translation.

Each entry's exact location in the manuscript is given below it, e.g. (NFC) S. 138: 462-3. The name of the pupil who collected the information, or the name of the teacher who transferred it into the logbook follows. These names are given just as they appear in the manuscript. Where an item is left blank or is illegible in the original that too is indicated in this transcription.

At the top of each entry, beside the title, the name of the school from which it came is indicated by a bold letter or letters, in brackets. For convenience, the name of each school has been given a shorthand designation, thus:

St Columbkille's N.S., Westport Quay – (Q)
Convent of Mercy Girls' School, Westport – (W)
St Patrick's N.S., Lecanvey – (L)

Pilgrims at the foot of the Reek.

Christian Brothers' N.S., Westport – (CBS)
Bouris N.S. – (B'r)
Kilsallagh N.S. – (K)
Teevenacroaghy N.S. – (T)
Brackloon N.S. – (B'l)
Murrisk N.S. – (M)

All the material from these schools has been transcribed and is being made available in the local libraries. This book contains a representative selection of entries under each heading, comprising about 50 per cent of the original material. It gives a good flavour of what is available as there is, of necessity, a degree of repetition from place to place in the original manuscript.

FOOTNOTES

1 http://portal.unesco.org/culture.

2 *Irish Times*, 17/9/1999.

3 Séamas Ó Catháin, 'Súil Siar ar Scéim na Scol, 1937-1938', in *Sinsear* 5, 1988, pp19-30.

Séamas Ó Catháin, 'Scéim na Scol', in *It's Us They're Talking About: Proceedings of the McGlinchey Summer School*, eds Margaret Farren and Mary Harkin (Clonmany, 1998).

4 An Roinn Oideachais, Irish Folklore and Tradition, Dublin, 1937.

5 http://www.ucd.ie/irishfolklore/english_html/schools.htm.

6 Index availble at http://www.mayolibrary.ie/localstudies.html.

7 *Mayo News*, 5 January 1938.

8 *Mayo News*, 20 February 1937.

9 *Mayo News*, 5 January 1938.

10 McNally, J., *Westport – The Smiles and The Tears* (Westport, 1998), p. 328.

11 'Mayo in the Twentieth Century', *The Mayo News* (December 1999), p. 58.

Background information for this introduction was gathered by talking to local people and from a number of valuable local publications:

The Mayo News Centenary Supplement, 2 March 1994.

Mayo in the Twentieth Century, *Mayo News Supplement*, December 1999.

Special thanks to Brónach Joyce, Clew Bay Heritage Centre, for her help in gathering and accessing information.

History of the Schools

Scoil Bhreac Chluain/Brackloon N.S.

The school opened as a one-roomed structure in 1849. It was one of three small schools established in the parish of Aughavale in the mid-1800s. The other two, Tiernacroaghy and Knappagh, have been closed. In the magazine published in 1999 to commemorate the school's 150th anniversary, An tAth. Micheál Mac Gréil recalled his own schooldays in Brackloon. He commenced school in 1936, one year before the senior pupils in the school commenced on their work for the Schools' Collection. This article gives very valuable information on the social and economic conditions of the time. Talking of the role of the school, An tAth. Mac Gréil says:

> When I was in Brackloon school practically all of those in the highest classes did not proceed to second level. The national school was first-second-and-third level as far as most were concerned. Those who attended regularly and were able to learn what was taught ended up with the basis of a very good education.

Brackloon School is justly proud of the contribution made by their pupils to the folklore project of the 1930s. Copies of the material submitted by the pupils then are held in the present school. In 1997 the school was completely refurbished.

The Principal teacher who supervised the folklore collection in 1937–1938 was Seosamh Ó Meachair.

Bó Ros/Bouris N.S.

In 1837 the Marquis of Sligo first made an application to the Commissioners for National Education for aid to build a schoolhouse in Bouris. After the original building was destroyed by fire, a new school was built in 1943 and opened to pupils in February 1944. There were sixty-three pupils on the roll then. The school was amalgamated with Louisburgh School in 1991, when there were eleven pupils on the roll.

The Principal teacher in 1937/38 was Breandán Ó Lionáin.

Scoil na mBráthar Críostaí/Christian Brothers' School, Westport

The school goes right back to 1824 when Fr Bernard Burke Adm., erected a schoolhouse at Castlebar Street under the patronage of Most Revd Oliver Kelly, Archbishop of Tuam and Parish Priest of Westport. This school came under the auspices of the Board of National Education. In 1835 Michael Harlow was the master and received £12 per annum from the Board and about £7 in local subscriptions. In 1865 the Christian Brothers took over the running of the school. The school had significant overcrowding problems and in 1962 a new primary school was erected on the Newport Road.

In 1987, when Coláiste Rís, the Christian Brothers' secondary school was opened, a commemorative magazine was published. Mr John Mulloy, who had commenced school in 1925, contributed an article recalling his experiences

Brackloon National School.

with the Brothers. He gives a very good picture of a child's life in Westport in the 1930s and mentions 'Br Healion', (C.I. Ó Haoláin), the teacher who was responsible for the school's contribution to the folklore survey. He says the teacher was 'burly and jovial, always with a twinkle in his eye', and he was held in high regard by his pupils.

Scoil Choill Sailigh/Kilsallagh N.S.

In 1833 the initial application was made to the Commissioners of National Education for aid to open a school in Kilsallagh. The school was amalgamated with Louisbourgh School in 1971 when there were fourteen pupils on the roll. The teacher then was Mrs Kathleen Morrison. The Principal teacher in 1937–1938 was Mairéad Bn. Uí Ghiobúin.

Bouris National School.

CLOCHAR NA TRÓCAIRE, LEAC AN ANFAIDH/ST PATRICK'S NATIONAL SCHOOL, LECANVEY

This school was opened to pupils on 4 December 1894. In 1895, fifty-five pupils were registered. In 1923, Canon Patterson of Westport invited the Ballinrobe Sisters of Mercy to Lecanvey to form a Branch House there and to take charge of the primary school there because the teacher, Mr Moran, was about to retire. The teachers who worked in the school before the Sisters took over in 1925 were Mr Thomas Moran and Mrs K. Tully. Sister Therese Conroy, who coordinated the Schools' Collection project here, taught in the school from 1927 until her untimely death in 1945.

SCOIL MHUIRISC/MURRISK N.S.

The original school in Murrisk was opened in a two-storey house in 1850, under the direct patronage of the Garvey and Buchanan families. The teacher's family lived on the ground floor and the school was held upstairs. A new school was

Christian Brothers' School, Westport.

opened in 1929. The Principal teacher in 1937-1938 was Seosamh Ó Cearbhaill.

Scoil Thír na Cruaiche, Thaobh na Cruaiche/ Tiernacroagha/Teevenacroaghy N.S.

This school was opened in 1848. It belonged to the Garvey estate and John Garvey built it to accommodate his tenants. Unlike all the other schools in the area which were managed by the priests of the parish, this school was managed by Garvey himself. It was a small school consisting of one room and a porch. The school closed in 1941 as a result of the small number of pupils attending it. In *Schooldays in the Shadow of Croagh Patrick*, Breezie McGreal, who had started attending the school in 1937, gave an account of her time there and of the last days of the school when the only pupils left were her sister and herself.

The Principal teacher 1937-1938 was N. Ní Mhóráin.

Kilsallagh National School.

Lecanvey National School.

Former Murrisk National School.

Ruins of Taobhnacroaghy National School.

Scoil Naomh Colmcille/St Columbkille's N.S.– The Quay School

When St Columbkille's School opened at the Quay in 1886, it replaced St Patrick's School, which had been in existence since 1855. Mr Jack Flatley who supervised the folklore collection here was appointed Principal in 1925 and held the post until he retired in 1962. He was then replaced by his wife Christina. A commemorative booklet was published to celebrate the school's centenary in 1986 and in it Mrs Flatley speaks of the nature of the school, 'St Columbkille's had a special identity of its own, an identity which was also taken on by the people of the Quay and gave the area a great sense of community.' The new school at the Quay opened in 1992.

Clochar na Trócaire, Cathair na Mart/Westport Convent of Mercy

The Sisters of Mercy arrived in Westport on 9 September 1842. One of their first actions was to commence the 'Poor School' on Castlebar Street, in a building that they first had to repair. The numbers attending the school soon grew from 100 to around 600 pupils. By the winter of 1845 a new 'Poor School' had been built. By 1850 the numbers had grown so large that there was need for an even bigger premises and the school was extended. In 1855 an Industrial School was opened.

In 1876 the final payments were made on a large new school building.

The Quay School.

This building was ninety years old in 1961 when it was 'condemned' by the Department and the new National School, St Patrick's National School, was built.

In September 2006, St Patrick's National School and the Christian Brothers' Boys School amalgamated under the name Scoil Phádraig.

The principal teacher in 1937–1938 was An tSr Bonaventure.

SCHOOLS, TEACHERS, PUPILS, INTERVIEWEES
BREAC-CLUAIN/BRACKLOON N. S. (B'L)

Reel S138. pp 341-514
Teacher: Seosamh Ó Meachair

Pupils:
Patrick Heraty
Sarah Heraty
Austin Kerrigan
Patrick Kerrigan
Thomas F. Maher
F. Mahon
Patrick Morley
Delia McGreal
Delia Walsh
Patrick Walsh

Former Convent of Mercy National School, Westport.

Interviewees:

Patrick Gibbons, Prospect
Peter Gibbons, Owenwee
Peter Gibbons, Treenlaur
Michael Heraty, Brackloon
Mrs Hearty, Owenwee
John Joyce, Owenwee
Thomas Joyce, Owenwee
John Kearns, Owenwee
Patrick Kerrigan, Owenwee
J. Maher
Tom McGreal, Brackloon
Ed McManus, Brackloon
Ed O'Malley, Brackloon
J. O'Malley, Brackloon
Pat O'Malley, Bohea
Thomas O'Malley, Owenwee
Peter Salmon
Patrick Walsh, Midgefield
Pat Walsh, Owenwee/Loughloon
Mrs Walsh, Midgefield

Bó Ros/Bouris N.S. (B'r)

Reel S138: pp 200–227
Teacher: Breandán Ó Lionáin
Interviewees: Bríghid Uí Ghrádaigh, Bairbre Ní Fhlaithbheartaigh

Scoil na mBráthar Críostaí, Cathair na Mart/ Christian Brothers' School, Westport (CBS)

Reel S138: pp 141–199
Teacher: An Br C.I. Ó Haoláin
Pupil: Gearóid Mac an Mhílidh
Interviewee: Pádraig Mac an Mhílidh, Sráid an Mhuilinn, Cathair na Mart

Coill Sailigh/Kilsallagh N. S. (K)

Reel S138: pp 228–276
Teacher: Mairéad Bn. Uí Ghiobúin

Pupils:

Margaret Burke, Kilsallagh
Janie(?) Gannon, Kilsallagh
John Gannon, Kilsallagh
Maggie Gannon, Kilsallagh
Pat Gannon, Kilsallagh
Mary A. Hester, Falduff
Willie O'Malley, Kinnock
Pat Scott, Kilsallagh
Mrs Gannon, Kilsallagh
Michael Gannon, Kilsallagh
Pat Gannon, Kilsallagh
Michael Gill, Kilsallagh
Mrs O'Malley, Kilsallagh
William O'Malley, Kinnock

Brackloon National School, 1920.

Brackloon National School, *c.*1930.

Delia and Joseph Maher, Brackloon, 1920.

CLOCHAR NA TRÓCAIRE, LEAC AN ANFA/CONVENT OF MERCY, LECANVEY (L)

Reel S138: pp 1-140
Teacher: An tSr Treasa

Pupils:

Jackie Cummins, Carramacloughlin
James Fair, Gloshpatrick
Tessie Fair, Gloshpatrick
Willie Fair, Gloshpatrick
Kathleen Farrrell, Lecanvey
Paddy Farrell, Lecanvey
Theresa Farrell, Lecanvey
Maggie Gannon, Carramacloughlin
Mollie Gannon, Carramacloughlin
Thomas Gavin, Carramacloughlin

Brother O'Mahony and CBS pupils in the late 1930s.

CBS pupils in the 1930s.

John Gill, Thornhill
Sal Gill, Thornhill
Peggy Lydon, Thornhill
Loreto Mortimer, Lecanvey
Mick O'Donnell, Gloshpatrick
Julie Agnes O'Malley, Lecanvey
Margaret Therese O'Malley
Therese O'Malley

Interviewees:

Austie Burke, Murrisk
Mrs Derrig, Kilsallagh, Carramacloughlin
Mr Fair, Gloshpatrick
Mickey Gavin, Carramacloughlin
Peter Geraty, Lecanvey
Myles Hynes, Carramacloughlin
Mr T. Moran
Mrs Katie Sammin
Thomas Walsh

Scoil Mhuirisc/Murrisk N.S. (M)

Reel S138: pp 515-554
Teacher: Seosamh Ó Cearbhaill

Pupils:

Máire Ní Bhrolcháin
Agnes Ní Ghabhainn
Máire Ní Ghrádaigh
Martan Mac Gréill
Máire Ní Ghrodáin
Meena Higgins
Máire Ní Mhóráin
Micheál Mag Réill
Eamonn Ó Rodaí
Seán Ó Ruadháin

Interviewees:

Austin Burke, Murrisk
Tom Gannon, Murrisk
Michael Gavin, Murrisk
Patrick Groden, Murrisk
John McGreal, Deerpark
Michael John Mc Greal
John Moran, Murrisk
John Reilly
Thomas Reilly, Murrisk
John Ruane, Murrisk
John Ruddy, Murrisk

Taobh na Cruaiche/Teevenacroaghy (T)

Reel S138: pp 277-340
Teacher: N. Ní Mhóráin

Pupils:

Austin Flanagan
Nora Flanagan
Mary McGreal
Marie McGreal

Interviewees:

Thomas Duffy, Boleybrian
Anthony Gavin, Scalp
Patrick Gibbons, Prospect
Mrs Patricia Gibbons, Prospect
Thomas Mc Greal
James Hastings, Crottmountain
Padraic Heraty
Dominic McGreal, Scalp
Michael McGreal, Scalp
Mrs McGreal, Scalp
Edward O'Malley, Owenwee
James O'Malley, Crottmountain

Past pupils of
Taobhnacroaghy and
Brackloon schools.

Mrs Margaret O'Malley, Owenwee
Thomas O'Malley, Owenwee

Scoil Naomh Colmcille, Westport Quay/St Colmcille's N.S., Westport Quay (Q)

Reel S137: pp 138-231
Teacher: Seán Ó Flaitile

Pupils:

Thomas Bourke
Kathleen Derrig
Peggy Eaton
Mary Gavin
Delia Gibbons
John Hastings
Ciara/Anna Hopkins
Dick/Richard Kelly
Tessie Kelly
Aidan McBride

Kitty McMullin
John O'Malley
Mary Ann O'Malley
Dolly Walsh

Interviewees:

Thomas Bourke, The Quay
Mrs Bourke, The Quay
Mrs Derrig, The Quay
Mrs Kathleen Eaton, Rosbeg
Eddie Gavin, Knockfin
Mrs Gibbons, Belclare
Mrs Hastings, Rosbeg
Mrs Hopkins, Rosbeg
Thomas Kelly, Clerihaune
Mrs Kelly, Clerihaune
Patrick Mac Bride, The Quay
Henry McMullin, The Quay
John O'Malley, The Quay
Mrs O'Malley, The Quay
Michael Walsh, The Quay

CLOCHAR NA TRÓCAIRE, CATHAIR NA MART/CONVENT OF MERCY, WESTPORT (W)

Reel S137: pp 232-277
Teacher: An tSr Bonaventura

Pupils:

Nancy Haran, Castlebar Road, Westport
Mary Geraty, Townranny, Westport

Interviewees:

Margaret Derrig, Westport Quay
Mrs Lizzie Geraty, Townranny, Westport
Mrs Eileen Haran, Castlebar Road, Westport.

John Haran, Castlebar Rd, Westport
Margaret Heraty, Carrowbawn, Westport
Mrs O'Malley, Ballinrobe Rd, Westport
Nellie Waters, Doon Castle, Westport

References:

Applications to the Commissioners for National Education for Grants, 1832–1890, National Archives Ireland.

St Patrick's Lecanvey, 1891-1991, Westport, 1991.

Schooldays in the Shadow of Croagh Patrick, Westport, 1999.

Westport Christian Brothers, *Special Celebration Book on the Occasion of the Official Opening of Coláiste Rís – December 1987*, Westport, 1987.

St Columbkille's National School (The Quay School), 1886-1986, Westport, 1986.

My Home Place

The name Lecanvey means 'Flag of the storm'; in Irish, Leac an Anfaidh. It well deserves the name as severe storms occur during the months of December and January…

Young and old had a great attachment to their home place. They knew and understood every aspect of that place; physical, cultural and historical. They knew the names of the fields, the names of the very stones and streams.

The home place was changing at the end of the 1930s. Due to emigration, there were fewer inhabited houses. The old thatched roofs were being replaced by slates. Fewer people spoke Irish as a vernacular, though some old people could still remember songs, prayers and stories in Irish. The common local surnames were well known in the small tightly knit communities where friendship and co-operation were the keys to happy and sustainable living. The Irish language was still in use in the names given to places and natural features and people could still understand what the names meant. They had memories of local roads being constructed and named, and memories too, of a time before those roads existed.

The familiar landscape was littered with the remains of the past, in the form of both ancient and more recent monuments. Graveyards were a focus for prayer and remembering the dead. Some graveyards incorporated very old wells which had traditional stations attached to them. These sacred places were still revered and the annual observances were still performed. People told legends about supernatural creatures such as a trout that could be observed in a local well – as a sign of luck, of the supernatural power therein – almost like the spirit of the well. Its violation would bring dire consequences for the perpetrators.

Formal education was valued highly in this culture. The precise sites of the first hedge schools were recalled, when people paid small money to be taught by a travelling teacher. In the late 1930s, the pupils collecting this lore had a unique opportunity to learn the make-up of their own place, just before those old ways, which had not changed for a very long time, gave way to a modern culture, more global in its proportions, more rational in its understandings.

My Home District

Owenwee (B'l)

The town land in which I live is Owenwee. There are 11 families in it. There are 62 people in it altogether. Kearns family is the most common. All the houses were thatched until a few years ago when they began slating them, and now there are five of them slated. Owenwee got its name from the river which is flowing through it. The waters of this river are yellow when in flood. There are seven people over seventy years living there. Thomas Joyce, Creag an tSionnaigh, can tell stories in English.

(S138: 462-3, Obtained by Sarah Heraty from J. Maher.)

1.1.1. Lecanvey (L)

Lecanvey is situated in the parish of Aughavale and in Murrisk Barony. In recent times the parish is often spoken of as Westport Parish. There are twenty-four families in the village and approximately 100 people. The most common family names are Mortimer, O'Malley and Geraghty. Most of the houses are slated at present. Within the last ten years the people got grants and loans with which they built new houses or repaired old ones.

The name Lecanvey means 'Flag of the storm'; in Irish, Leac an Anfaidh. It well deserves the name as severe storms occur during the months of December and January. Six old people over 70 live at present in the village. Two, namely Mrs Mortimer (Marie Gill, maiden name) and Mrs Toole tell old stories in English. They are mostly connected with the fairy forts and local pisreoga.

Houses were not more numerous in former times than at present, as Lecanvey was in Lord Palmer's estate and so was spared the horrors of eviction.

(S138:93, An tSr Treasa.)

1.1.2. Thornhill (L)

Thornhill is situated in the parish of Aughavale and Murrisk Barony. About 13 families live there, approximately seventy people. The family name most common is Gill. Like Lecanvey the people availed themselves of the grant and have built a number of slated houses. Only a few thatched roofs still remain. The town land got its name from a large clump of blackthorn bushes which grow on a hill in the village.

The following people over seventy years live in the village: Mickey Gavin, Mrs Gill (Mary Murphy), Jimmy Gill, Joseph Gill, Pat Needham. Mickey Gavin tells stories and speaks Irish fluently. He tells that he learned his Irish by listening to his parents conversing with the neighbours. When his father and mother wished to talk in private they spoke Irish. The children were generally sent to an adjoining room or put out to play. Mickey, being curious, sometimes listened and picked up words here and there. Later on he would ask his mother the meaning of this word and that. Having a good memory, he was able to retain a good knowledge of the language.

Houses were more numerous in this village long ago. Some of the owners were evicted.

(S138:94-5, An tSr Treasa.)

1.1.4. Gloshpatrick (L)

Gloshpatrick is situated in the parish of Aughavale, in the Barony of Murrisk. About 54 people live there. No two families of the same name live there. Names of existing families: Fair, O'Donnell, Kelly, Moran, Gannon. All the houses are slated now. A few old thatched ones remain but are used as outhouses. The village got its name from a little stream which flows by Glosh graveyard into Clew Bay. Only one man over 70 lives there now. He is Mr Thomas Moran, a former teacher in the school.

Houses were more numerous here in former days. At one time previous to

Lecanvey church.

the evictions, more than 200 families lived in Glosh. The little village had a few streets; Sráid Mhór (Big Street) and Sráid na Madaí (Street of the Dogs) were two of them. Others were Sráid an Mhuilinn (Mill Street) and Sráid an Tobair (Street of the Well). As a result of the famine the people were unable to pay the rent and on 4 April 1859, 200 families were evicted by the 'Crowbar Brigade'. Most of them emigrated to England and America.

The town land is famous in history from its connection with St Patrick. His blessed well is still there but not frequented as a place of pilgrimage nowadays. (S138: 95-6, An tSr Treasa.)

1.1.5. *Carramacloughlin (L)*

Carramacloughlin is situated in the parish of Aughavale in the parish of Murrisk. Eight families live in the village, about 40 people. Three thatched houses remain. The others were slated recently. The town land got its name from a man called O'Loughlin who lived there long ago. The place was called 'O'Loughlin's Quarter'. Evidently this man's descendants must have emigrated. No one of the name lives there now.

One old man over 70 named Thomas Walsh lives there. He can speak Irish and tell stories. Long ago there were 50 houses in the village. After the bad times several families went to America. The most common name is Gavin. (S138:99, An tSr Treasa.)

1.1.6. *Murrisk (M)*

The name of my home district is Murrisk. The town land is Carrowkeel, the parish is Aughavale. There are a lot of families in Murrisk. The most common names are Grady and Gavin. All the houses are slated now, but in former years all the houses were thatched. There are not many ancient ruins in my home district. There is a ruin of an old abbey where the Augustinian monks lived long ago. The inside grounds of the old abbey is a graveyard now. There are not many old people in my home district now. The majority of them know Irish and they can tell various stories of olden times in Ireland. Grainne Uaile the sea Queen of the West was baptised in Murrisk Abbey. There are many names of rocks and fields in my home district. There is a place called Log na nDeamhan (Serpents' Hollow) in at the foot of Croagh Patrick, where St Patrick banished the serpents long ago. (S138: 546, Told by Michael Gavin, sixty-five, farmer, Murrisk, to Agnes Ní Ghabhainn.)

1.1.7. *Durlas (B'r)*

Tugtar an t-ainm úd thuas ar an mbaile atá (taobh) thoir ón scoil, mar gheall ar sheandún atá ar thalamh Sheáin Uí Sgathghaoil ar an mbaile sin. Durlas nó dún cloiche a bhí ann, lena linn. Deir na seandaoine go bhfaca siad féin soithigh cloiche ann fadó le linn a n–óige, ach níl aon tuairisc orthu sin anois.
(S138: 227, B. Ó Lionáin.)

Translation:
Durlas is the name given to the town land which is east of the school, because of the old fort which is erected on the land of John Scahill. It was a 'durlas' or stone fort that was there. The old people say that they saw stone vessels in it long ago when they were young, but there is no sign of them now.

1.1.8. *Faghburn (T)*

The name of the town land in which I live is Faghburn. It is in the parish of Westport and the barony of Murrisk. Part of the town land is in a valley over which there is a hill covered with rocks. This is how the town land got its name. There are fourteen families in the town land and a population of forty-eight. The

Gloshpatrick Well.

family names most common are McGreal and Walsh.

The most common type of houses are thatched, but there are two slated houses and two with sheet iron. The houses were much more numerous in former times than at the present day. Some of the old people died and then some of the young people sold their lands and went to America.

(S138: 322, Collected by Nora Flanangan, Scalp, from Anthony Gavin, Scalp, Westport, aged seventy-six, 6.10.38.)

1.1.9. Rosbeg (Q)

My home district is in the town land of Rosbeg, in the parish of Westport, and barony of Murrisk. There are about twenty-six families living in Rosbeg. The houses are mostly slated but there are a few old thatched houses. There are no old people living in Rosbeg now. In olden times there were more people in the town land, but through hard times the people had to emigrate to England and America. The town land is not mentioned in any song or saying.

(S137: 200, John Hastings, Rosbeg, Westport. Obtained from Mrs Hastings, forty-three, Rosbeg, Westport.)

Gloshpatrick Well.

1.1.10. Westport (Q)

The name of my district is Westport. There are about 1,500 families in the town land and there are about 3,500 people living there. The most common family names are O'Malleys, Gavins, Walshes, Morans, Gradys, and McGreals. Slated houses are the most common type. Long ago there were a lot of beeves exported from Westport. On this account it was called Cathair na Mart – 'The City of the Beeves'.

(S137: 201, Kathleen Derrig, The Quay, Westport. Obtained from Mrs Derrig, forty-six, The Quay, Westport.)

PLACENAMES

1.2.1. Local Placenames (W)

There are traditional tales told about many places in the Westport district and one of these places is Doon Castle.

Doon Castle is said to be built hundreds of years ago but it is not known who built it or for what reason. It was said that the Kings of Connaught resided there for a while and fought many battles round it.

Sheeaune Hill is a very high hill with a mound on top and it is said that the fairies have their dances and parties on the rath there.

Drummindoo has taken its name from a graveyard in which babies are buried. 'Druim an Dubh' means the ridge of the graveyard. 'Dubh' is an old Irish word for graveyard.

Townranny is a place a half mile from Westport, on a hill. In that place there is a ring of trees and grass growing inside. It is said that fairies dance there at night.

Ardygomman Wood is about a mile outside Westport, below the railway. There is a small wood here and people were buried here that died of hunger during the famine days.

Knockfin – Cnoc Fionn near Aghavale, Cathair na Mart. It is believed locally that Fionn Mac Cumhaill was buried in the hill or mound in Knockfin.

(S137: 233-5, Nancy Haran, Castlebar Rd. Told by Mr John Haran, Castlebar Road, Westport.)

1.2.2. Local Placenames (L)

Four or five fields in the village bear the name Fiodán (watercourse). Near them a kind of tunnel crosses the road bringing the water of a mountain stream to the sea. A number of fields bearing hillocks here and there are called Crigán, corruption of Cnuican (?). The fields beside the sea are called Pullinga – probably from poll (a hole). A flat level field in the village is called Currach (wet bog). Other names are Páirc Ard (high field), Lecarba (?), Cnoc na Leice (flat ground here), Ceathrú (¼ acre field), Sraith Cathaoir, which gets its name from the fairy fort called Cathaoir. There are a few English names, like Meadow Field, Long Field, Black Ground Pastures. The streams and hollows have no particular names.

(S138: 42-3, An tSr Treasa.)

1.2.3. Local Placenames (M)

Murrisk is situated beside the sea, about six miles to the west of Westport. As its name tells us, it is beside the sea, muir meaning the sea, and uisge the water. It is at the foot of Croagh Patrick, or Cruach Phádraig, the hill of St Patrick where St Patrick spent forty days and forty nights praying and fasting on top of the mountain. Before St Patrick came it was called Cruachán Eagla [*sic*], or the Eagles' mountain because the eagles used to live there. At that time most of it was covered with woods.

The small road leading to Croagh Patrick is called Bóthar na Míos [*sic*], or the road of the dishes. It probably got that name because there used to be a Pattern in Murrisk, in a field near the road. The people used to cook food at the Pattern and eat it from dishes.

To the North East of Murrisk the sea comes in, in some places and forms deep holes in the land. This is called Murrisk na bPoll or Murrisk of the holes. To the West there is a long stretch of sand reaching out into the sea. This is called Bior Tráigh or the point of the strand. Near this there is another piece of land stretching out into the sea. This is called Cathair na Ranna. There was supposed to be a fort here long ago, but there is no trace of it now.

Clew Bay itself was called Cuan Modh. A sort of king, Aengus, built a fort in an island. This was called Inis Modh. Hence we have Cuan Modh.

Cathair na Rann got its name from a chieftain named Rann who had a fort there. It is a big piece of land and it is near the sea.

Páirc Láir is the middle field. Páirc Mór is a big long piece of land and it is near the sea. Páirc na Céibhe is a piece of land where there is a well.

Log na nDeamhan is so called because St Patrick is supposed to have vanished [*sic*] the serpents from there. Log an Aifrinn is so called because Mass was said there in the Penal Days.

Cloch mhór is a big rock which is near the river. Cloch sgoilte is a big rock up in the hills. It is a split rock.

Creag buí, Sidh rua, Cruach Phádraig and Creagán Ard are big hills. Cruach Phádraig is a very high mountain where St Patrick prayed forty days and forty nights. Sidh rua is so called because there was supposed to be a fairy living there. Log na gCaorach is the hollow of the sheep.
(S138: 552-4 , S. Ó Cearbhaill.)

LOCAL ROADS

1.3.1. Local Roads (B'l)

Bóthairín Fhéilim is a road leading to the Owenwee bogs. The first portion of it was made about a hundred years ago, and some time later it was made about two miles more into the heart of the bog. This was done to accommodate turf cutters.

Owenwee road is leading from Brackloon to Carraig. The first piece of it was made about a hundred years ago, and it proceeded further about twenty years ago. All the other roads are made so long that there is no recollection of the date. Before bridges were made in the district, rivers were crossed by means of fords. Átha Mhór in Cloona is the biggest ford in the locality. There is a Mass path leading to a Mass rock in Bohea.
(S138: 461, S. Ó Meachair.)

MONUMENTS AND RUINS

1.4.1. Local Monuments (B'l)

There is a stone in Bohea about one hundred yards west of Nugent's house and about fifty yards from the Leenane Road. There is a cross carved out on this stone. The old people say that there is a priest buried there. The stone was erected in honour of this priest.

There are three stones in Brackloon, about a hundred yards from Kelly's house. The people say that there are three giants buried there. There are strokes written on them.
(S138:495, Collected by Margaret Kelly, Brackloon, from Ed. Kelly, seventy, Brackloon.)

1.4.2. *Crois Leac an Anfaidh (B'r)*

Sa bhliain 1830 thóg Maitias Mac Domhnaill, seanathair Shéarluis Mhic Dhomhnaill, athair mná Uí Laoideáin, an fear ar leis an talamh, an chrois agus an túr atá ar aghaidh theach pobail Leac an Anfaidh, ar an gcnocán ó thuaidh, i gcuimhne 'Acht Shaoirse na gCaitliceach', 1829. Tá an túr déanta i bhfoirm croise, agus tá crois adhmaid fascaithe ina mhullach.

Is léir, le breathnú air, gur le saothar fear agus in aonturas, a rinneadh an cnocán go bhfeicfí an túr agus an chrois i bhfad ó láthair.

(S138: 226, B. Ó Lionáin.)

Translation: The Lecanvey Cross

In the year 1830 Matthew Mac Donnell, the grandfather of Charles Mac Donnell, father of Mrs Lydon, the man who owned the land, erected the cross and the tower which are opposite the church in Lecanvey, on the hill to the north, in memory of the Act of Catholic Emancipation, 1829. The tower is built in the form of a cross, and a wooden cross is erected on top of it.

To look at it, it is clear that the small hill was built up manually and for the purpose of making the cross visible from a long way off.

1.4.3. *Local Monuments (L)*

In Gloshpatrick graveyard there were a few old stones with peculiar marks and strokes on them. It is not possible to decipher what language they are in. The flags were taken some time ago by the County Council and put in a tunnel near Belclare river. Some of the local people were not too pleased over this, as they reverenced the flags from their connection with the graveyard.

(S138: 128-9, An tSr Treasa)

1.4.4. *Poll a'Chapaill (Q)*

Beside Lord Sligo's demesne in Westport there is a house now occupied by Mr Carrol. At the back of this house there is a hole which is supposed to be bottomless. It got its name from a tragedy that occurred there. A horse and cart backed into it. The man, in trying to save the animal's life, fell in himself.

At that time, it was the custom for the women of Westport to wash their clothes in a river or in a pool of water. One day a woman was washing her clothes in this pool. She spread the clothes on the stones and beat them with a beetle. She found great difficulty in washing a certain garment. She believed in charms and she brought out the cat. The cat jumped into the hole and vanished.

Then she had no trouble in washing the clothes. As she was preparing to go home, she removed one of the stones. Under this she found a pot of gold. The old people say that some of the houses now standing in Westport were built with this money.

There is a fence around this hole now for safety. The woman's name was Mrs Talbot. She has friends still living at the Mall, Westport.

(S137: 143-4, Thomas Bourke, The Quay, Westport. Obtained from Thomas Bourke, fifty-four, The Quay, Westport.)

GRAVEYARDS

1.5.1. Old Graveyards (B'l)

There are four graveyards in this parish: Treenlaur, Bohea, Aughavale and Drummin. Treenlaur is situated a mile and a half south west of this school. Bohea is a half mile south of this school. Drummin is south west of this school, about four miles. Aughavale is north of this school about two and a half miles.

Treenlaur is a round grave. Unbaptised children were baptised in it and now

Bohea stone.

it is used for a pen for sheep.

Bohea is still used for burying unbaptised children. It is not [a] level graveyard and bushes are growing on the south west of it. There is a blessed well here also and St Patrick's Rock is here.

Drummin graveyard is shaped like a square. The church is in the middle and there are bushes growing all around on the fences.

(S138: 508, Collected by Sarah Heraty, Owenwee, from Thomas O'Malley, about seventy, Owenwee.)

1.5.2. Local Graveyards (K)

There are only four graveyards in my parish: Kilgeever, Oughavale, Glosh and Murrisk. Kilgeever graveyard is situated under the foot of Kinnock Hill. It is square in shape. There are the ruins of a church standing still. There is a blessed well in the graveyard. Some people come from far away to perform a station. The station is performed by going around the well five times barefooted, saying five Our Fathers, and five Hail Marys each time. You finish up by saying a few prayers for the dead.

(S138: 264-5, Mr Michael Gannon, Kilgeever.)

HOLY WELLS

1.6.1 Tobar Phádraig – Fuirreagal (B'r)

Tá Tobar Phádraig, nó a lorg ba chirte a rá, suite ar thalamh Phádraig Mhic Oireachtaigh i bhFuirreagal, míle ó dheas den scoil.

Tá sé suite i bpáirc ar a dtugtar 'Páirc a' Mhiolla', mar gheall ar an seanreilig le haghaidh gasúr óga ar a dtugtar 'Miolla'. Tá sé ag bun an chnoic agus ar bhruach an pharóiste. Bhíodh dhá sceach mhór, ceann ar gach taobh, ag béal an tobair, ach níl ann anois ach ceann amháin – an ceann atá taobh ó dheas. Bhíodh balla cloiche timpeall ar an tobar agus é ag oscailt ar an taobh thoir, ach tá sé tite anois nach mór. Bhí urlár leac ar an tobar ón mbéal siar go dtína dheireadh.

Ní thugtar an turas lá ar bith áirithe, ach, de réir mar a chloisim, an lá ab fhearr a d'fheilfeadh don duine. Is ag iarraidh leighis do dhaoinibh agus do bheithigh a bheadh tinn a thugtar an turas.

Ar an gcoirnéal thoir-ndeas den reilig, ar thaobh an chnocáin, tá carnán cruinn cloch ar a dtugtar 'An Altóir'. Is ag an altóir seo a thosaítí an turas. Tá cúig cinn déag de chlochaibh cruinne duirlinge, tuairim is chomh mór le dorn dhuine, leagtha ar an altóir. Siúladh an duine 15 uaire timpeall an tobair, d'abraíodh

Bohea stone.

sé 'Ár nAthair' agus 'Sé do bheatha Mhuire' gach uair dá dtéadh sé thart, agus comhairigh na huaireanta leis na clocha ar an altóir.

Deich slata fichid siar ón Altóir, ar thaobh an chnoic freisin, tá cloch mhór a bhfuil poll mór domhain cruinn ann. Tá an poll tuairim is deich n-orlaigh ar leithead agus cúig orlaigh doimhin. An lá a chonaic mise é bhí sé lán d'uisce, ach deirtear liom go mbíonn sé tirim san aimsir thirim. Siúladh an duine a bheadh ag tabhairt an turais trí huaire timpeall ar an gcloch seo, ag rá 3 'Ár nAthair' agus 3 'Sé do bheatha Mhuire' lena linn sin dó. Ansin siúladh sé ó thuaidh 20 slata go dtí an tobar agus d'abraíodh an Páidrín ar a ghlúnaibh i mbéal an tobair.

Bhí piast bhán insan tobar agus dá mbeadh leigheas i ndán don duine nó don bheithíoch a bhí tinn, d'fheicfí an phiast ag snámh thart ar thóin an tobair. Ach mura mbeadh leigheas i ndán don othar, ní fheicfí aon amharc ar an bpéist, nó dá bhfeicfí féin is ag imeacht as amharc a bheadh sí.

Thugtaí abhaile cuid den uisce agus thugtaí le n-ól don othar é. Nuair a bhíodh an turas tugtha ag an duine, ba ghnách ofráil éicint a thabhairt ag an tobar. D'fhágadh na mná bioráin gruaige, nó bonn coiscrithe, nó rud éicint den tsórt ann. Boinn, nó seanscabaill, nó pingin, a d'fhágadh na fir ann.
(S138, 205-6, B. Ó Lionáin.)

Translation: Patrick's Well – Furgill (B'r)

St Patrick's Well, or the trace of it which would be the more proper thing to say, is situated on the land of Patrick Geraghty in Furgill, a mile south of the school.

It is situated in a place which is called 'Páirc a'Mhiolla', because of the old children's graveyard which is called 'Miolla'. It is at the bottom of the hill and at the edge of the parish. There used to be two big bushes, one on each side, at the mouth of the well, but now there's only one – the one to the south side. There used to be a stone wall around the well which was opened on the east side, but it has almost fallen now. There was a flag floor at the well, from the mouth all the way back to its rear.

The 'turas' is not made on any particular day, but, as I hear, on the day that best suits a person. The 'turas' is made to ask for healing for people or animals which are sick.

At the south-east corner of the graveyard, on the side of the hill, there is a round pile of stones which is called 'The Altar'. The 'turas' was begun at this altar. There are fifteen round gravel stones, about as big as a person's fist, placed on the altar. A person must walk fifteen times around the well, saying the Our Father

Kilgeever Well.

and the Hail Mary every time they go round, and they count the rounds with the stones on the altar.

Thirty yards beyond the altar, on the side of the hill, there is a big stone which has a big wide circular hole in it. The hole is around ten inches wide and five inches deep. The day I saw it, it was full of water, but I am told that it is dry in the dry weather. The person who is making the 'turas' must walk around this stone three times, while saying three Our Fathers and three Hail Marys. Then he must walk 20 yards north to the well and he must say the Rosary, while kneeling at the mouth of the well.

There used to be a white serpent in the well and if the sick person or the animal were destined to be cured, the serpent/worm would be seen swimming around at the bottom of the well. And if no cure was in store for the patient, there would be no sign of the serpent/worm, or if it were to be seen it's going away out of sight it would be.

Some of the water from the well would be brought home, and the patient would be given it to drink. When the person had completed the 'turas', some offering would be made at the well. The women would leave hairpins, or holy medals, or something of that kind. The men used to leave a medal, or an old scapular, or a penny, there.

Kilgeever Well.

1.6.2. Holy Wells (W)

There are two Holy Wells in our parish of Aghagower. St Anne's Well is in Cushloch and St Patrick's Well is in Aghagower. People visit St Anne's well in the Summer and also in the Autumn.

A station is performed there, thus: On the rock, people say seven Our Fathers, seven Hail Marys, and seven Glorys, and the Creed. Then they creep from the rock down to the gate and they say five Our Fathers and five Hail Marys. Then they get seven stones and go round the well outside seven times and drop a stone each time. When this is done, they wash their feet in a river nearby. They creep then from the gate into the well and go round it three times and each time they say one Our Father and one Hail Mary. Then they kneel down beside the well and drink three drops of the water.

This station has to be done on three days. When the station is finished people make offerings at the well and they also leave relics at the well.
(S137: 248-9, Nellie Waters, Doon Castle, Westport.)

1.6.3. Our Holy Wells (T)

There are four Holy Wells in this district. St Patrick's Well is on the side of Croagh Patrick. It is said that St Patrick used this well during the period of forty days which he spent on the mountain. There is also another well in a village called Bohea which is connected with St Patrick. St Brigid's Well is in Kilgeever and people go there on the fifteenth of August to do stations. People always leave something at the well when leaving it. St Colmcille's Well is in Aughagower. There is a stone wall built around the well and there is a high tree overshadowing it. It is said that someone caught a fish in this well and when he was roasting it on a tongs, it jumped out and into the well again, with the mark of the tongs on its back. Anyone who asks a request at this well will know it is granted if the fish comes up to the top of the water.

People who suffer from pains or diseases of any kind rub the affected part with the water of these wells.
(S138: 311-2, Collected by Mary McGreal, Scalp, Westport from Mr Michael McGreal, fifty-four, Scalp, Westport, 17.5.38.)

1.6.4. Our Holy Wells (B'l)

There is a holy well in Bohea about three quarters of a mile from this school, 100 yards from the Leenane Road. This was discovered about ten years ago by Patrick Kearns, Glynsk, he having heard it from his grandfather. No stations or prayers said there. Shrubs all round it.

There is another blessed well in Aughagower about two miles from this school. People still visit it to perform stations by going around it seven times saying any prayer they like. It is said there was a trout in this well and he used not to come out to anyone only those who performed their station right. Very long ago this trout was caught and brought home, put on the tongs to roast; he jumped off it and made his way back to the well and the track of the tongs on his side. In 1920 the British soldiers caught him and killed him so he never escaped again. It is thought that this trout lived there for hundreds of years.
(S138: 464, Obtained by Patrick Morley from John Kearns, Owenwee.)

OLD SCHOOLS

1.7.1. Old Schools (K)

Along the side of the road in Martin O'Malley's field, beside the big bush, there was a hedge school. The master used to get very little wages for his work, only what the people would collect for him. A slate and a sharp stone they had for writing and sometimes they would have a quill pen. The class of ink they used to have was made out of soot and water. They were not allowed to speak Irish or learn it. Mr Grady was the master for the district.
(S138: 242-3, John Gannon, Kilsallagh.)

1.7.2. Hedge Schools (T)

Hedge schools were not very plentiful in my district at any time, yet there were some in it one time. Their local name was 'School-house'.

The children went to the houses of those who were able to teach them and sat on low stools in the kitchen. The principal subjects taught were reading, writing, arithmetic and catechism. They did sums with slate-pencils on slates, and they wrote with quill pens and ink. The children were taught Irish catechism also. The teachers were paid by some people with money, and others gave them food for payment. Some gave potatoes, and others gave fowl, each according to his means.
(S138: 282, Collected by Mary Mc Greal, Scalp, Westport, from Mr Thomas Duffy, Boleybrian, Westport, 18.11. 37.)

Home and Hearth

The oldest type of dwelling which is remembered to exist in this district was a small house made of sods. The roof was also made of sods and beams of bog deal were laid across under the sods which acted as a means of support to the roof … There are thirteen spinning wheels in the district here; five in Lecanvey, five in Carramacloughlin, and three in Gloshpatrick.

On the eve of the Second World War the cultural and physical landscapes were changing. The old traditional thatched houses were giving way to new dwellings which would last right up to the present day. House change was the outward marker of the profound cultural changes that would take place during and after the war period. The young people's parents and grandparents were able to recall the very old way of life, before houses even had a chimney.

The diet was simple and unvaried, heavily reliant on potatoes and oatmeal. The special meals associated with festive times such as Hallowe'en were eagerly anticipated and enjoyed. They provided relief from the daily round of plain fare, however wholesome that might have been. Bread was baked daily on the open fire, from wheat flour ('shop flour') and Indian meal (ground maize meal). Potatoes were used as a staple, even in bread making, for boxty and potato cakes. Oaten bread or oat cakes, made from ground oatmeal, was an important part of the diet. It was eaten every day and was also carried by travellers, either on journeys at home or on the emigrant journey, to ward off the 'féar gorta', the terrible, debilitating hunger that could kill a person if they had nothing with which to stave it off.

Butter making was one of the high points of the weekly round; once a week in winter, and sometimes twice a week in summer. The yellow butter was as precious as gold and traditional beliefs and customs, both pagan and Christian, were used to protect it from harm.

The community was self-sufficient in many ways. In addition to food, they could provide their own candles, baskets, iron and metal goods, ropes, etc. Their sheep provided the wool to be spun, dyed and turned into articles of clothing. The forge was a central place in the community and the smith played a vital role in respect of agriculture, transport and the carriage of goods. But some local forges were closing at this time and people would have to travel farther and farther to avail of the smith's services.

Many houses still had a spinning wheel, but people were beginning to buy their clothes from shops, except for men's shirts. which were still being sewn at home from material bought in the shop. People knew how to dye the spun wool, drawing on the rich lore of plants and their respective dying properties. Baskets were not today's expensive craft objects, to be prized as pieces of vernacular art, or even as sculpture. They were practical, utilitarian objects used for fetching and carrying everything from turf to potatoes. There was no plastic yet. While some people were undoubtedly gifted at basket-making, everyone knew how to make a 'cleeve' from sally rods, to serve their own needs. Lime was quarried and burned, in a complex process, to enrich the land. The men who burned the lime earned every penny of the five shillings they received per barrel for the finished product. Like the other crafts of the time, lime-burning requires skill, patience and hard work.

Younger people were now wearing shoes, and sometimes clogs. But there were still some old people who did not wear shoes all the time and who remembered how important it was to take good care of the unprotected feet. They called 'Huggy! Huggy!' as a warning to the fairies when they were disposing of the water in which they had washed their feet. This little Irish phrase, 'Chugaibh! Chugaibh!' (literally 'To you! To you!') was a shard from a past culture, fossilised in this protective ritual.

DWELLINGS

2.1.1. Old Houses (B'l)

Houses were thatched long ago. This thatch was got and cut on the mountain. All the old houses had a bed in the kitchen. It was placed at one side of the fire and it was called the cailleach. The fireplace was always at the gable. Glass was not in the houses long ago; [it was] stone and wire that were used instead of glass. The chimneys were made of wattles and clay. Floors were made of clay and sand and flags. Half-doors are common in this district still. Fire stuff was turf, scraws and wood. The light at night was bog deal splinters and candles. Candles were made locally.
(S138: 502, Collected by Delia McGreal, Owenwee, from Dominick McGreal, fifty-five, Owenwee.)

2.1.2. Dwellings (T)

The oldest type of dwelling which is remembered to exist in this district was a small house made of sods. The roof was also made of sods and beams of bog deal were laid across under the sods which acted as a means of support to the roof. The roof was thatched with rushes or sedge to keep the sods from getting wet. There was a hole in the centre of the roof which supplied the place of a chimney. This type of chimney was plastered with clay. These dwellings went by the name of botháin.

There was only one apartment in these botháin and all the furniture which belonged to a bedroom had to be kept there. It must have been a very uncomfortable task to crush everything into a small apartment like this.

The next kind of dwellings were common houses made of stones, some of which exist at the present day. The roofs of these houses were made in much the same way as the botháin, except that the chimneys were plastered with clay and lime and thatched on the outside with rushes. These chimneys were usually on the gable end of the kitchen. There were generally two rooms in these houses. Sometimes there was no glass in the windows, only a hole in the side wall with a door on it which they closed at night or when it was raining. Those houses had clay floors, which certainly would not present a very pleasant appearance on a wet day.

Sometimes there were two doors to those dwellings, and along with the front door there was a half-door which was left closed while the front door was open.

Rosbeg, Westport.

The domestic animals such as cows and horses were always kept in the kitchen at night, but they were driven out to the pastures in the morning and brought back again in the evening, just as they are brought back to the barns nowadays.

The means which they adopted for giving light at night in former times was not very convenient. Sometimes they used bog deal splinters, sometimes common candles, and sometimes rushlights. The rushlights were peeled rushes twisted together and dipped in sheep's tallow. These were also called dips. Nowadays none of these kinds of light are used as the people have got oil lamps which show much better light than those candles.

(S138: 292-4, Collected by Mary McGreal, from Mr Anthony Gavin, seventy-eight, Scalp, Westport.)

FURNITURE

2.2.1. Old Furniture (K)

Long ago the old people used to have a chair made out of straw for a bed. Each person would have a separate one for himself. The kind of cups were wooden noggins. The kind of chairs they used to have were made out of rods. They would boil them in a pot until they would change colour. Then they would make the chairs out of them. Sometimes they might get a plank in ashore. If they would, they would employ a man for one day to make stools and chairs out of it. They had also another sugán chair called a boss. It was made with a straw rope and a stick.

(S138: 265, Mr Michael Gannon, Kilsallagh.)

FOOD

2.3.1. Food in Olden Times (Q)

Long ago people used to have two or three meals a day. Rich people who could afford it had three meals but the poor people had only two meals. The breakfast which was the first meal was eaten early in the morning. People who had cows to look after and other work to do did not have their breakfast until they had all the outside work done. Porridge was eaten for breakfast. Some people liked milk with it and others preferred butter and sugar. They had boxty, cally, cabbage, bacon and potatoes for the dinner. Sometimes they had turnips for the dinner. On Fridays they had herrings and cally for the dinner. If they had milk they drank it, but if not, they used water. The people drank more buttermilk long ago than they do now. For that meal they had, they also had potato cake. The supper was eaten at night before going to bed. They had boxty, potato-cake, oatmeal bread, bran cake, and yellow meal cake. Sometimes they had tea at one of the meals. The oatmeal bread was made from oatmeal, water, and salt and it was baked before the fire.

Long ago the people hardly ever ate fresh meat. Pigs' cheeks was the kind of meat that was eaten. They killed their own pigs and cured them. The people ate a lot of vegetables long ago. On Easter Sunday people had a goose or a turkey for the dinner. They ate a lot of eggs on that day also. On St Martin's Day they always had some kind of fowl for the dinner. They used to have a special tea on November night. They used to have a big feast on Christmas Eve. They always had a goose for the dinner on Christmas Day. They used mugs or saucepans called porringers to drink from long ago.

(S137: 167, Delia Giblin, Belclare, Westport. Obtained from Mrs Giblin, forty-seven, Belclare, Westport.)

BREAD

2.4.1. Bread (K)

Long ago the old people used to make different kinds of cakes. They used to make oatmeal cakes with water and oatmeal and bake them before the fire. They used to make potato cakes with potatoes and flour. They used to make Indian meal cakes. They used to wet it with water or milk and bake it on a griddle. They used to put oatmeal and Indian meal cakes on a leaf of cabbage and put another leaf over them and leave them on the hearth on small coals until they would be baked.

(S138: 252, Mr Michael Gannon, Kilsallagh.)

2.4.2. Bread (L)

For special occasions a sweet cake used to be made in olden times, generally for Christmas Day and New Year's Day. Pancakes are made too for Shrove Tuesday night and Hallow Eve. The vessel in which these cakes were, and are still made, is called a pot-oven. When fuel is scarce the oven is put in a hanging position over the fire and a few coals placed on the lid. With a good fire, it is put on the brand iron, either triangular or round-shaped iron stand. Gríosach (hot ashes and embers) is put underneath the oven and red coals on top to bake it.

Part of a quern is in one house in the village, John O'Malley's, Lecanvey. The children's parents have not seen querns being used, but the fathers and mothers remember the old people speak about them. Evidently they were used in the district in days gone by.
(S138: 124, An tSr Treasa.)

2.4.3. Boxty (L)

The children are quite familiar with Boxty Bread. It is made as follows. Raw potatoes are grated first, on a coarse grater, generally made from an old tin can with holes pierced through it, by means of a coarse long nail. The potato is rubbed up and down on the coarse surface. The grater is placed over a clean basin or pail and the pulp allowed to fall into the vessel. This watery mass is put into a clean white cloth, generally a flour bag, and squeezed thoroughly. [I have seen this squeezing done in South Galway by putting the tongs across a pail and squeezing the cloth full of pulp down on the bars.] There is left now dry pulp in the flour bag, and starchy water in the clean vessel. The water is allowed to set. It is poured off and the starch left behind is used for starching cottons, linens, etc.

The dry pulp is put on the losset, a little flour shaken through, and a small drop of water, just enough to moisten it. It is kneaded, something like ordinary bread, and shaped into a round cake, salt being added beforehand. The round is cut up into triangular pieces and baked on a griddle. The bread has a dark appearance but tastes nicely with butter.
(S138: 130-1, This information about bread-making was given by Stds 5,6, and 7.)

CHURNING

2.5.1. Churning (B'l)

I have a churn at home. It is a dash churn and is about three feet tall. It is one and a half feet wide at the top and about two at the bottom. The upper half is called the caisín and the lower the body…

[It is] the woman of the house that mostly does the churning. When the churning is going on, if a stranger comes in, he helps in the work for fear he would bring the butter with him when he would be going home. It takes about a half hour to churn it sometimes. The churning is done by hand. The churn dash is always moved upwards and downwards, and when they are taking out the butter, they roll it from side to side. When the butter is made it gathers in lumps on top of the milk. Water is poured on it sometimes. Hot water is put on it when the milk is cold, and cold (water) when it is too hot. The butter is lifted out with the claibín which is a little wooden bowl with a hole in it. It is then washed with water. They then salt it and make it into prints.

Before churning they put a burned coal under the churn.

They bless themselves with salt and then shake it on the dasher, three times.

Sometimes when it would take a long time to make a churning, they used to make a gad of a hazel rod and put it around the dasher on the lid.
(S138: 477–8, Collected by Austin Kerrigan, Owenwee, from Patrick Kerrigan, sixty-five, Owenwee.)

2.5.2. *Churning (L)*

There are three types of churn: dash churn which is the most common, machine churn and barrel churn.

The majority of the children are familiar with the dash churn. The parts are the dash – round piece of wood with holes here and there; a long handle is fastened to it, which the worker moves up and down. The lid fits in about 8 or 10 inches from the top. There is a hole in the middle through which the dash passes. A little piece of wood is near this hole to act as a handle for the lid. There is a small wooden cup with a circular hole in the bottom, put down through the dash handle. It keeps the cream from dashing out too quickly. It is called the clabaire.
(S138: 114–15, An tSr Treasa. Information under this heading was supplied by Stds 5,6 and 7.)

CRAFTS

2.6.1. *Old Crafts (B'l)*

There was candle-making carried on in this district long ago. They made them out of tallow and rushes. They used to peel the rushes, and melt the tallow, and keep rolling the rush in it till the candle was formed. Basket and cliabh-making was also carried on, and is up to the present day. Osier rods are used. Spades, gates, fire cranes, parts of ploughs, harrows, etc. were manufactured by P. Joyce, Liscarney. Scraith chloch (rock lichen) was used for dyeing. It was got growing on rocks. It was then boiled in water in a pot until it was to its perfect colour. Ropes were made also out of tuighe-bualach (tuighe-buarach?). First of all they pull the rushes and boil them in a pot. They then leave them out in a sunny place to dry. They plait them then into ropes.
(S138: 441, Obtained from Mrs Heraty, Owenwee.)

THE FORGE

2.7.1. *Local Forge (B'l)*

There are two forges in this district. One of them got broken about fifteen years [ago] and the other since last year. Pat Lyons, Liscarney, and Harry Hughes of Lanmore were the smiths. Hughes is a young smith but Lyons is there for many a year. These forges are situated beside both a stream and a crossroads. The forges have thatched roofs. The door is an ordinary one. There is one fireplace in each of them.

   He [the smith] uses a sledge, hammer, rasp, knife and anvil, wedge, vice, tongs. He shoes horses, asses, and jennets. He makes ploughs, harrows and a spade which is called a láighe. He shoes wheels in the open air. Forge water is a cure for sore eyes and warts. Smiths were always looked upon as being very strong. (S138:480, Obtained by Sara Heraty, Owenwee, from John Joyce, seventy-five, Owenwee.)

2.7.2. *Forges (K)*

There are two forges in the parish. The names of the owners are Michael Duffy, Kilsallagh, and Michael Gavin, Murrisk. Mr Duffy's father and uncle were smiths also. Mr Duffy's forge is situated near the road. Mr Gavin's forge is situated near the public road to Westport. The forges are built of stone and roofed with sticks and thatch. The door is made of wood like any door. There is only one fireplace in the forge. The bellows was not made locally.

   The implements which the smiths use are: a hammer, a sledge, a pincers and a rasp. He makes no implements such as harrows or ploughs. (S138: 252-3, Mr Michael Gannon, Kilsallagh.)

2.7.3. *The Local Forge (T)*

There are three forges in this district, two of which are not in use. These two are in the village of Liscarney, and the forge which is being used is in Murrisk.

   The man who owned one of the forges which is not in use has left it recently and gone to England. The man who owned the other one was shot in the year nineteen hundred and twenty one by the Black and Tans. The forge which is in Murrisk is owned by a man called Patrick Garvin.

   Those forges have thatched roofs and in the side wall there is a square about as big as a window with a shutter on it. This serves as a window. There is also a door on each forge, much the same as the door of the common dwelling house.

(S138: 299-300, Collected by Mary McGreal, Scalp, from Mr Michael McGreal, fifty-two, Scalp, Westport, 7.4.38.)

BASKET–MAKING

2.8.1. How a Cleeve is made (L)

First a big green sod, about 2 feet square, is cut. The sod is left on bare ground. There are three rods put down at each corner of the sod and two are put down in a vertical position, every three or four inches apart. When all the standing rods are in position, the weaving is begun. Fine rods, sally or hazel, are woven in and out between the standing rods. The weaving is begun at the bottom and continued upward until the centre is reached. Here there are openings left called 'eyes', to serve as a convenience in lifting the cleeve. The weaving is continued to the top. Here 'the hanging' is put on. It is made of two or three rods twisted together. Sometimes a piece of rope is attached to the hangings to help the

Jim Lavelle, blacksmith,
Mill Street, Westport.

workman in carrying the cleeve on his back.

The bottom of the cleeve is the last part that is made. It is constructed from basketwork, like the four sides. It is generally so arranged that it can be loosened at three sides. The load (turf, wrack) slips down easily without removing the cleeve from the donkey.

(S138: 32-3, Written by Paddy Farrell, Lecanvey, Westport.)

2.8.2. Basket-making (L)

The baskets are used for carrying turf from the rick, for picking potatoes, for straining cooked potatoes, turnips and mangolds for pigs, etc. To strain, the basket is placed across a tub or keeler; the boiled potatoes, water and all, thrown in. Sometimes two small wickerwork handles are put on the basket, either at the sides or on crossbar and opposite semicircle.

(S138: 33-4, Boys of Stds 5 and 6 gave this account of basket-making.)

SPINNING

2.9.1. Spinning (L)

The usual preparations for the making of woollen threads are as follows. The first thing to do after shearing the sheep is to wash the wool. When it is dried, the woman of the house starts her work. She teases the wool, by drawing it out between the hands, and removes any bits of sticks or dirt which would cause difficulty in the carding. Then the wool is greased, generally with paraffin oil, so that it will not break in the spinning.

Next, the wool is carded. The cards are two even pieces of wood with handles and steel teeth. When the wool is put in between, and the cards pulled in different directions, the wool becomes fine. The wool is then taken off and made into a roll on the back of the card. When a number of rolls are made, they are left on the stock of the spinning wheel.

When the wheel is ready for the woman to spin, she puts in a spindle and round that she fastens a piece of wool. Then she turns the wheel with the right hand, and while turning she pulls the wool with the left to make it even. When one spindle is filled she puts in another. Sometimes she doubles the thread for stockings. The thread is also used for woollen jerseys. Occasionally women send thread to the weaver and out of it he makes blankets. The weaver in this locality lives in a village called Mullagh. His name is Pat McDonnell.

(S138: 34-5, An tSr Treasa.)

DYEING

2.10.1. *Dyeing the Thread (L)*

In this district the people make dye from herbs or weeds. A pretty green dye is formed from the roots of dock leaves. Dye is also got from certain kinds of seaweed, principally scraith fliuch (scraith chloch[?,] rock lichen). It is used to colour woollen goods. When articles of clothing, jerseys etc., are made from the white homespun wool, they are scoured first and then dyed. The roots, weeds, etc., are boiled with a certain amount of water in the dye-pot and the dye is allowed to cool. The white articles are put into the dye, allowed to soak well, boiled again, and then hung out to dry. Some houses had a dye-pot, a large metal pot kept specially for making the dye.
(S138: 35, Written by Therese O'Malley.)

2.10.2. *Dyeing (K)*

This is how brown dye is made. They get scraith chloch off the rocks with a knife. They boil it in a pot and they put onion peels through it. Then they put in whatever they have to dye. When it is boiling an hour, they lift it and wash it, in hot water, and they leave it out to dry. Then it has a good brown colour.
(S138: 230, Mary A. Hester, Falduff, 15.3.1938.)

2.10.3. *Dyeing (K)*

Long ago the women used to dye the wool black and make cloth out of it. They used to get airgead lóchra (airgead luachra – meadow sweet). That is a white flower that grows plentifully along hedges. They boiled this for hours in a pot. It coloured the water a brown colour. This was called bark. When it was well boiled they strained off the water and put it back into the pot again. They put the wool into it, and also a substance called "bog ink". They got the "bog ink" in a certain place in the bog. This gave a good black colour to the water and a lasting dye to the wool. Seldom they bought dye in the shop.
(S138: 232, Maggie Gannon, Kilsallagh, 16.3.1938.)

CLOTHES

2.12.1. *Old Clothes (K)*

The men long ago used to wear báiníns made of flannel. The women used to spin and card the wool and get the weaver to weave it. They used to wear frieze trousers made of wool and coloured with bog wood and bog ink. They used to wear frieze coats also. The women used to wear a dress of flannel coloured brown and they would get it pressed. The body and skirt would be sewn together. They used to wear strong nailed shoes and their own make of stockings. They used to wear cloaks, and robes on them, made of the best material out of the shop. They used to wear white caps with three rows of lace border around the edge of them. They would only wear these clothes to Mass. Everyday they would wear a black or a red coloured petticoat and their skirts pinned up. They would wear marine (?) petticoats as underwear to Mass and a row of black braid around the bottom of them. The children would wear [illegible] dresses.
(S138: 238-9, Maggie Gannon, Kilsallagh.)

2.12.2. *Clothes Made Locally (L)*

There are no tailors in this part of the parish. Most of the clothes are bought ready-made.
Shirts are made in the homes from material bought in the shops. Flax wasn't grown locally, as far as can be ascertained.

Socks and stockings are knitted in the home. So also are the jerseys for boys and girls. The thread is spun at home. There are thirteen spinning wheels in the district here; five in Lecanvey, five in Carramacloughlin, and three in Gloshpatrick.

When a man dies, his wife doesn't wear a hat for a [blank] or more. She wears instead a black shawl. This is done to show respect for her husband's memory.
(S138: 117-18, An tSr Treasa.)

BURNING LIME

2.13.1. *The Lime is Burned (L)*

Lime is burned frequently in Lecanvey village. The limestone is got at the seashore and is quarried first. This is done by breaking the stone into small pieces with a stone-hammer and sledges. It takes three or four days to break enough of

Spinner and donkey with panniers.

stones to fill the limekiln.

The limekiln is filled in the following way. The men put a line of turf about two or three feet in depth, to set the limestone on fire. The next line consists of the broken stones, about four barrowfuls are required for this. The next line is turf, the next stones, and so on until five lines of each are in the kiln. After this, the men put on either slack, coal, coke or cinders. The next two lines are stone and turf again.

When it is filled to the top, or 'water measure' as they call it, they get scraws. These are built round with stone and turf in the middle. Next they get a couple of ass loads of turf and throw them into the face of the kiln. With this they put a bucket of red coals, and in a half hour or so it is on fire. It is left all night burning.

In olden days people had to stay up during the night, but this is not necessary now as the kiln is large, and enough of stones and turf are added to last till morning. They have to rise early and keep the fire burning all through the day. The fire is not quenched for four days.

The lime is sold by the barrel to the people of the district. The cost at present is about five shillings per barrel.

(S138:36-7, Written by Therese O'Malley, Lecanvey. The child's father, John O'Malley, has a limekiln.)

CARE OF THE FEET

2.14.1. Care of Feet (B'l)

Long ago people used never wear shoes until they would be sixteen or twenty years of age. The children of the present day go barefoot in Summer and Autumn. Dirty water should not be thrown out on the threshold at night, because there is a woman under it, and if you wet her she will curse you. If people have to throw out water at night, they should say, 'Huggy! Huggy!'

We have no shoemakers or cobblers in this district.

(S138:479, Obtained by Paddy Walsh, Owenwee, from Pat Walsh, fifty-five, Owenwee.)

2.14.2. Care of the Feet (L)

In former times children didn't wear boots until twelve or thirteen years old. One old lady goes barefoot still, even in Winter. She is over seventy. Children go barefoot in Summer, but wear boots all Winter.

Boots are made and repaired locally. The trade is a tradition in the family of

Limekiln, Fahburren.

shoemakers here. The one shoemaker in the district is dumb. The trade has been a tradition in the family for generations.

Clogs are made at Westport Quay. They were worn by farm labourers in olden times. Poor children wear them at the present time. There are no records of leather-making in the district, nor foot coverings of sheepskin or of untanned hide.
(S138: 116, Written by Loreto Mortimer, Lecanvey, Westport.)

2.14.3. The Care of the Feet (T)

There are accounts of people who never covered their feet with anything heavier than 'woollen stockings'. These stockings were made without any soles. They were kept in place by a loop in the upper part to put in on the middle toe. This footwear went by the name of troighthín. They wore these troighthíní in the months of February and March. They were not worn to keep out the cold but to save their feet from what they called "Woreach" (bórach – having crooked or ill-shaped feet[?]). The feet used to crack with the cold weather and these stockings were a great protection.

Our forefathers were very superstitious and they had strange beliefs about many things. One of these was to throw an old shoe after a girl on her wedding day. They believed that this would bring her good luck.
(S138: 289–91, Collected by Mary McGreal, Scalp, from Mr Michael McGreal, fifty-six, Owenwee, Westport. 2.2.38.)

The Land

When Our Lord was dying on the cross, it is said that the robin came and tried to pull the nails out of his hands and feet, and while doing so a drop of blood fell on his breast and that is why the robin has a red breast ever since.

In 1930s Ireland the economy was still largely rural. People were growing crops and tending animals on their own mixed farms. To be successful in this enterprise required an abundance of local knowledge, honed by generation after generation in one place, in a process of constant, continuous observation and refinement.

The care of the animals, for example, required, not just practical husbandry skills, but also knowledge of the traditional prayers and blessings used to protect them from harm. Each species of animal had its own familiar call. These calls are like a kind of inter-language between humans and their domestic animals in this part of the world. They betoken the intimate bond between the two, over a long period of time. Poultry too played an important role in the rural economy. Eggs were a good source of protein, and a good way to earn cash when they were sold. The poultry themselves were also a significant food source, both for home consumption and for sale.

The potato crop was still crucially important in the diet. Great pride was taken in growing the crop to maximum effect, and very precise local knowledge was involved in the process. Most of the work associated with cultivation was still being done manually and some of the particular terminology used was still in the Irish language. Certain varieties of seed potatoes were favoured for the particular circumstances of soil and climate. Here, then, is a body of expertise and survival skills in which people took much pride, coaxing the best possible crop from land that was difficult and challenging.

As for the other common plants, aside from crops and vegetables, some were known only by their Irish names and no English language equivalent was available. While English was employed in large areas of people's lives at this time, agriculture was one of the last areas to submit to the anglicisation process. Indeed some plant names may never have yielded, and where the names are still recalled at all, it is probably in a variant of the Irish form.

There are also interesting indications of the traditional medicinal applications of some of the common plants, though it seems a great pity now that there is not any detailed description of the actual method in which a plant would be used to effect a cure. Perhaps the youth of the pupils militated against their ability and interest in collecting such material, or perhaps the traditional knowledge was already beginning to fail at this stage.

Much lore was found concerning the common wild birds in the district. Birds such as the corncrake, which is now endangered, are here mentioned with no intimation that they could ever become scarce, let alone extinct. As well as the factual information about the birds, their habits and habitats, people knew stories, beliefs and weather lore associated with them.

When it came to reading the weather, there was a huge bank of locally observed phenomena to draw on. Earning their livelihood from the land and the sea, this information was of vital importance to the community. Every aspect of the natural environment could be used as a weather indicator, even though it seems that rain might have been the most likely outcome of most of the signs available! In addition to their local lore, people could recite 'The Signs of Rain', a little poem published in school readers at various times. It was composed by Dr Edward Jenner (1749-1823), the person who developed a vaccine for smallpox.

Surprisingly perhaps, this chapter on rural life is relatively short. Nevertheless it contains a wealth of lore which is of local value, and which illustrates the great changes which have come about in the interim. At present, the inhabitants of these villages have little need for the rural knowledge and skills recorded here. But, we cannot know if such particular local information will ever again be important. If it should be required, for whatever purpose, whether practical or historical, it is lodged safely here, giving testimony to a vibrant rural community living in harmony with nature and able to provide for the majority of its everyday needs.

FARM ANIMALS

3.1.1. *The Care of Our Farm Animals (L)*
The domestic animals are cows, horse, donkey, pigs, sheep, cats and dogs. When driving the cows the people say, 'Whurish' 'Whurrish'. When calling cows or calves they say, 'Suck' 'Suck', or 'Prigee' 'Prigee'.
(S138:112, This information was written by Stds 5, 6 and 7.)

3.1.2. The Cowhouse (L)

The Cowhouse is arranged as follows. A long pole or stick runs parallel to the wall, about 1½ feet in height and about 4 feet from it. This is the manger in which the hay is placed. The low manger is for the calves. Staples are placed in this thick pole and a chain to tie the animals. For the cows a different tying is adopted. Long poles about 4 feet apart are nailed to the rafters and fastened to the floor. To the side of each post there is a long iron staple. Into this a fairly long piece of chain is fastened. To this the tying proper is attached. An 'S' hook joins the tying together. The chain goes up and down on the long staple as the cow moves her head. The tying chain consists of two pieces.

When the people have finished milking the cows, they take some of the milk on the thumb and make the sign of the cross on the animal's hip. While doing this, they say, 'Bail ó Dhia uirthi', or 'God bless her'. When anyone comes into the cowhouse while the milking is going on, he says, 'God bless the work', or 'God bless the cows and the people.' The answer is 'The same to you.'

The manger for the horse is raised higher from the ground than the one for cows. It is always above the horse's knee. The manger is called a rack. The horse is cleaned with a curry comb and brush. The hair is clipped with a clippers.

The following are the sounds used to call the animals. For the horse 'Puch' 'Puch'; the sheep 'Shough', pronounced like 'how' with 's' before it. To call the pig the people say 'Furish' 'Furish'. There is a special call for the different kinds of fowl. For geese 'Baddy' 'Baddy'. The last 'dy' gets a sound like 'thee'. For ducks

Croagh Patrick from Bertra beach.

'Fweed' 'Fweed'. For turkeys 'Bee' 'Bee' 'Bee'. For hens 'Tuk' 'Tuk'; for chickens a sound like 'Dís' 'Dís', the 's' like 'sh', and 'í' fada.

The eggs for hatching are marked with a cross. This is done in a very primitive fashion. A cipín (a small stick) is rubbed up and down on the soot of the chimney, and it is with this cipín the cross is made. There are two reasons, first to bring luck, and secondly to see which eggs have birds, e.g. when a neighbour gets eggs to set from another, she only marks her own and leaves the others minus a mark.

(S138: 112-4, An tSr Treasa. This information was obtained from Stds 5,6 and 7.)

3.1.3. Farm Animals (Q)

When the farmer is calling the cows he says, 'Puig, puig', and he calls the calves by saying, 'Suck, suck.' When he is calling the horse, he says, 'Pough, pough.' He calls the sheep by saying, 'Shoun, shoun', and the pig is called by, 'Muc, muc', or 'Hurrish, hurrish.'

St Bridget's Cross is hung over the cowshed door to keep away disease from the cattle. Some cows give more milk if you sing while milking them. Cows are very wise and soon get to know who milks them and if a stranger comes to milk them, they very often refuse to give milk to him. They also know the correct time for milking and when that time draws near they generally let the farmer know by lowing or moving their hooves. When people are finished milking they make the sign of the cross on the cow's back with milk. This is said to be lucky. It is usually done by old people.

Cats are generally kept in farmers' houses. They also have pet names such as Daisy, Bell, Ginger and Fluff, but they are often called Puss.

Farmers keep a lot of fowl. These fowl are hens, chickens, ducks, geese and turkeys. In big farms the fowl have a field in which to stay during the day, but in smaller farms they are generally kept in a railed-in plot. Some people train their fowl to come when someone whistles or shakes a bucket. The fowl are also called by names. Hens and chickens are called by saying 'Chuck, chuck.' Ducks are called by 'Quack, quack', or 'Bathie, bathie', and geese by saying 'Geg, geg.' Turkeys are called by saying 'Pee, pee.' Fowl are very useful and they do not give a lot of trouble.

(S137: 184-7, Tessie Kelly, Clerhaune, Westport. Obtained from Thomas Kelly, fifty-eight, Clerhaune, Westport.)

POTATO CROP

3.2.1. The Potato Crop (L)

All the small farmers of this district sow potatoes each year. They plant one or two acres. Their holdings are very small, from 4 to 7 acres.

Saving the Crop

Most farmers plant in ridges and the work of preparation is done with the spade or láighe as it is locally called. I have only seen one farmer here using a plough. When potatoes are sown in lea land, the farmer scores the land in the following way. He gets some thatching twine and two sticks. He fastens one stick in the ground and winds some of the twine round it, securing it carefully. Then he takes the rest of the twine and draws it along whatever length he requires his ridge, making sure to keep it straight. He fastens the second stick in the ground, winding the twine round it. Next he turns up a green scraw straight along by the scoring line. This is called the fóidín. When the fóidín is complete the scoring line is raised and changed about 1½ feet. Another fóidín is dug now and the space between the two is called the shough or dyke. The line is changed again leaving a space of 4 feet this time. This is usually the width of the ridge. Two more fóidín, 1½ feet apart are dug as before, another ridge then, and so on until the required number is there.

All the scoring is done and ridges marked out before manure is applied. Then wrack, black wrack, is put down first on the green sward of the ridge. Over that, stable manure, and sometimes over that, fertiliser or shop manure, when the land is poor. The slits, i.e. the seed potatoes, are now spread across the ridge about a foot apart each way. The slits are next covered with clay.

Sometimes the potatoes are sown on the double, that is one man covers half the ridge one side, another the other side. They go in opposite directions. They usually go over the work a second time to dress the brows, that is to flatten down the side of the ridge with the spade. The name liaghán for the part of the potato left when the slit is cut is quite common here. The way they express preparing the seed is "We are cutting slits." Scoring is done also on land where a crop has been the year before. The land here is sodden, damp land. Late potatoes grow better than early ones.

Sticking Potatoes

This method of growing potatoes is used in small gardens. The ridges are scored in the usual way. Then the farmer sticks the spade into the clay, and at the back of it he inserts a slit, covering it with clay. The manure is put on when the little stalks appear above ground. This method holds good for small gardens where the soil is fairly rich. Most of the work here is done with the spade. The spades are bought in the local shops. It is not customary here for neighbours to help one another in farming work. A farmer who hasn't enough of men has to hire workers.

Moulding and Spraying

When the little green stalks appear above ground they are moulded. This is done with the spade or shovel. The clay is put round the young stalks and occasionally bag manure is added. May is the month for this work. When the stalks are higher any weeds in the ridges are pulled out, and in June or early July the crop is sprayed. The spray is a mixture of bluestone and washing soda. A large barrel is filled two thirds with water. A flat board is placed across the mouth; the bluestone is put in a coarse bit of canvas, tied to the board and allowed to sink partly under the water. To this liquid the melted washing soda is added. The spray is put on with the budget which is strapped on to the worker's back. There is a [illegibile] at the side, moved up and down, which scatters the spray on the stalks. The primitive method of spraying with the heather broom still holds in occasional small gardens in this district.

Digging and Storing

Early potatoes, of course, are dug in the end of June or early July. When the old people see new potatoes for the first time they say, "Go mbeirimid beo ag an am seo arís." Late in October and early November, the main crop is dug and secured. The digging, like the sowing, is done with the spade. The children pick them. As they pick, they sort, by gathering the big, good potatoes first in baskets and cleeves, and leaving the partly black ones, póiríní and sunburned ones on the ridge. Later these are picked and boiled for pigs or fowl. The good potatoes are left for a time in bags until they dry and then they are pitted. The pit is triangular shaped. When the dry potatoes are heaped over one another, they are covered with rushes or straw. Over this, clay is put, and at the mouth of the pit they put green scraws.

   The kind of potatoes sown are Epicures, Kerr Pinks, Champions (which grow best here), May Queens, Arran Chiefs and Arran Banners.
(S138: 101-4, An tSr Treasa.)

3.2.2. The Potato Crop (Q)

The various kinds of potatoes sown in this district are: Early Roses, Flounders, British Queens, Irish Queens, Kerr Pinks, Champions, Epicures and Up to Dates, and Aran-Chiefs. Early Roses and Flounders are the earliest potatoes. Kerr Pink are the best potatoes for the land in this district.

(S137:188-190, Delia Gibbin, Belclare, Westport. Obtained from Mrs Gibbin, forty-seven, Belclare, Westport.)

HERBS

3.3.1. Herbs (B'l)

The following are the harmful weeds that grow in this district.

Fearabán (buttercup) is very harmful. It spreads very rapidly and makes the soil poor. It grows both in bad and good land, and impoverishes every crop. It is never used as a cure.

Chickweed is found in good land. It spreads very rapidly. It makes the land

Potato-pit.

poor. When boiled the juice will cure a sore throat.

Devil's Bit is not harmful but it spreads fairly rapidly. It does not make the land poor and it only grows in good land. When bruised up it is a good cure for sores such as boils.

Airgead Luachra (meadow-sweet) is found in bad land. It does not spread rapidly and is not very harmful. It is not used as a cure for any purpose. It grows between one and two feet in height and wears a silver-coloured flower. When boiled and strained the juice can be used for colouring white cloth black.

Mountain Sedge is not harmful. It does not spread very rapidly. It only grows in bad land around rocks. When this is boiled, the juice is very good for purifying the blood. It is not used for any other purpose.

Smearment grows in the bog. It does not spread and is very hard to be found. It grows about six inches high and wears a silver-coloured flower. When boiled the juice can be used as hair oil. It is never used for any other purposes.

The Penny Leaf grows in a wall. It does not spread very rapidly. It only grows in stone walls. When this leaf is heated, it is good for drawing bad stuff out of sores. It is about the same size as a penny.

(S138: 465-6, Collected by Paddy Morley, Owenwee, Brackloon, from John Joyce and others.)

3.3.2. Herbs (T)

Many plants grow on the farm, some of which are harmful and some of which are very useful. The most harmful ones are the hemlock, the dockin [dock], the créachtar [créachtach?, loosestrife/crane's bill], the botharlán [buachalán?, ragwort], the celestring [celandine?], the willow-weed, the fearabán [butttercup], the thistle and the clúbhán [?].

The hemlock is a green weed which produces a white flower in Summer. It grows about a foot from the ground and is supposed to be very poisonous. The celestring is green and produces a yellow flower in Summer, and is very harmful in grass. The dockin grows very close to the ground and is also very harmful in grass. The willow-weed is a red, seedy flower which grows chiefly in vegetables.

There are also many plants which are cures for certain complaints. The foxglove is good for a sore throat. This plant is red and grows a foot from the ground. From the dandelion, wine can be made. This is good for rheumatism. The chicken-weed, as well as being harmful, is also a cure for a swelling on the neck. Likewise, the hemlock is a cure for swelling on horses' feet. The airgead lóchramh (airgead luachra – meadow-sweet) is a white sweet-smelling flower which gives a black dye. These are the most important herbs which grow on

the farm.
(S138:314-15, Collected by Mary McGreal, Scalp from Mr Thomas O'Malley, fifty-nine, Owenwee, Westport. 14.7.38.)

BIRD LORE

3.4.1. Bird Lore (B'l)

The birds commonly found in this district are wild duck, wild goose, snipe, curlew, grouse, swallow, corncrake, hawk, blackbird, cuckoo, woodcock and robin. Boys are told if they rob a bird's nest, the bird will curse them. If swallows are seen flying high it betokens good weather, but if they fly low it betokens bad.

When Our Lord was dying on the cross, it is said that the robin came and tried to pull the nails out of his hands and feet, and while doing so a drop of blood fell on his breast and that is why the robin has a red breast ever since.

One day Our Lord was passing where a hen and a duck were feeding. It was raining and Our Lord went in under the hen's wing to let the shower pass, but the hen picked him. So he had to go in under the duck's wing. The duck left him there and he made her feathers grow in such a way so as not to let water touch her skin.

If a blackbird chirps at night it is a sign of snow. A March cock will crow at night. The Bean Shee (Bean Sí) is a bird which cries after certain families.
(S138: 446-7, Obtained from Patrick Kerrigan, Owenwee.)

3.4.2. Bird Lore (L)

These are the wild birds commonly found in the district: blackbird, robin, thrush, starling, plover, wagtail, sparrow, wren, yellow hammer, jackdaw, magpie, hawk. The usual common sea birds seen in Clew Bay are: seagull, cailleach dubh, curlew. A little bird, greyish brown with red feet, is found here along the shore. Natives call it the redshank. The migratory birds are the cuckoo, corncrake, and swallows, including house martins. Grouse are found among the mountains, snipe in the marshy places.

The robin builds its nest in a mossy bank – very near a work of art. The blackbird and thrush build in the forked branch of a tree, or high hedge. The wren builds in a wall, with hay, wool and moss. The nest is so small that your two fingers could scarcely go into it. The crows and jackdaws build on top of a tree or in chimneys. They use sticks and wool. The magpie builds on top of a

Saving hay at Rosbeg

tree with sticks and wool. He is a great thief and sometimes steals clothes pegs, even knives and spoons to his nest. The swallows and martins build in eaveshoots. Some of the swallows here build in the cliff. They repair the old nests, making them from mud. The curlews build in the cliff too. The skylark builds on the ground, so too does the corncrake.

The children here believe that it is very unlucky to rob a nest, or touch eggs. They hold that if a boy robs a nest, a curse will follow him. If one touches the eggs, they believe that the bird will forsake the nest. (I am glad to say very few nests are robbed here. The children respect the little birds.)

When the curlew cries and flies towards the hills, it is a sign of stormy weather. When the swallows fly high, fine weather is expected; when they fly low bad weather is expected. When the seagulls come in on land, a storm is expected. A crowd of magpies foretell rain. When the wren hides in a hole in the wall, we may expect snow.

The old story of the robin's kindness in taking the thorns from Our Lord's head is well known in the district. It is also said that a little bird follows the cuckoo and waits on her. The bird is called the riabhóg (pipit).

Boys imitate the blackbird's whistle and the thrush's song. All the children love to imitate the cuckoo. They take an interest in the habits of the birds and always announce when they see the first swallow or hear the cuckoo.

(S138: 44-5, These notes about birds were written by Stds 5,6, and 7.)

Weather Lore

3.5.1. *Weather Lore (K)*

Black clouds moving quickly across the sky is the sign of rain. The south-west wind brings most rain. When the birds fly high, it is the sign of good weather. But when they fly low it is the sign of bad weather and rain. When the sea is foamy, it is the sign of bad weather and storm. Dust on the road is also the sign of storm. Fog is the sign of frosty weather and sometimes rain. Smoke is the sign of good weather, when it goes up straight in the sky. Flies bring bad wet weather. When blue light is in the fire, wet weather is coming. The dog eats grass when wet stormy weather is coming. When soot falls it is the sign of bad wet weather. (S138: 249-50, Mr Michael Gannon, Kilsallagh.)

3.5.2. *Weather Lore (L)*

The following is a list of local beliefs with regard to the weather.

(i) *Signs in the sky*:
When the sky is dotted with stars which sparkle and glisten it is a sign of frost.

When the sun sets in a bank of red clouds it is a sign of good weather, but when the clouds are copper-colour it is a sign of rain.

A dark inky sky indicates snow or heavy rain.

When there is a halo round the moon, and when she "sits down", it is a sign of broken weather.

If weather is bad when a new moon appears, then it is likely to continue bad for the month. Should the weather "take up" (to use a local expression) with the new moon, fine weather may be expected.

The common verse about the rainbow is well known here – 'fisherman' is substituted for the word 'shepherd', probably on account of the nearness of the sea. 'A rainbow in the morning is the fisherman's warning; a rainbow at night is the fisherman's delight.'

It is a local belief also that when the sky is red in the east or south-east we may look out for a storm.

(ii) *The wind at certain points*:
When the wind blows from the east or south-east, a local saying puts it, 'When the wind blows from "Log na nDeamhan" look out for a storm.' The word Lecanvey means 'the flag of the storm', and certainly it is no leasainm (nickname). South-east is the worst point, though occasionally west and south-west winds

Ploughing with horses.

are bad enough in their own way. With the west and south-west winds the rain accompanies the storm. The natives prefer this wind as the force of the rain lessens to some extent the severity of the storm. A north wind foretells snow, hail and very cold weather.

(iii) Birds and Animals as Weather Omens:

When the seagulls fly from sea in on the land in large flocks a storm may be expected. When the curlews screech loudly it is a sign of broken weather. When the swallows fly low it is a sign of rain and when they fly high it is a sign of fine weather. When the wild geese fly low it is a sign of rain and when they fly high it is a sign of fine weather. When the hens pick at their feathers rain is expected. When the ducks flap their wings up and down it is a sign of rain. When the geese fly for a fairly large distance, natives say it is a sure sign of a coming storm.

When the dog eats grass we may expect rain. When the cat turns his back to the fire it is a sign of rain. The cattle turn their backs to the black clouds and seek shelter before the rain falls. When they run to the farm and prance about excitedly a storm is brewing. When the sheep run to the wall to seek shelter, bad unsettled weather is expected. When we see the cows grazing on the hills early in the morning, we say expect a spell of fine weather. When the cattle run to the shade of the trees or try to cool themselves in pools and shallow streams, heavy oppressive weather is at hand.

Westport Quay

(iv)Natural features:

A red sky in the early morning indicates bad weather. A mackerel sky in the middle of the day is a sure sign of rain before night. There is a big rock in Clew Bay close to the pier. It is called Carraigín Dilisc by the natives. When the white waves break near the rock it is a sign of bad weather. When the hills appear near, bad weather is expected. A dense fog on the Reek, with a west wind, foretells rain. When the haze leaves the top and rests at the base of the mountain, fine weather is expected. When the dust rises in clouds from the roadway, rain will follow.

At Lecanvey, being a seaside place, the sea is a great indicator of the weather. When the sea is green it is a sign of bad weather. When it is dark and rough a storm is brewing. A blue sea, calm and tranquil, indicates a spell of fine weather.

When the flies gather thickly on window panes, especially after cold weather, it is a sign that fine weather is at hand. When midges are very busy on a summer's evening, great heat is expected.

When the cattle are annoyed by the cuileoga (horse flies), it is a sign of great heat.

The bat foretells fine weather when he flies about in the dusk or twilight.

(v)Fires and smoke:

When the smoke goes up straight it is a sign of frost and also of fine weather. When the curling smoke ascends from the chimney, broken weather is expected.

Different colours in the flame of the fire indicate bad weather. Streaks of blue in the "gríosach" indicate rain. When the soot falls in large lumps we may expect rain.
(S138: 18–21, An tSr Treasa.)

3.5.3. *Signs of rain (Q)*

The soot falls down, the spaniel sleeps,
And spiders from their cobwebs creep.
Last night the sun went pale to bed,
The moon in halos hid her head.
A boding shepherd heaved a sigh,
To see a rainbow span the sky.
The walls are damp, the ditches smell,
Closed is the pink-eyed pimpernel.
Loud quack the ducks, the peacocks cry,
The distant hills are looking nigh.
Hark how the chairs and tables crack,
Old Betty's joints are on the rack.
The frog has changed his yellow vest,
And in a russet coat has dressed.
(S137:160, Peggy Eaton, Rosbeg, Westport. Obtained from Mrs Eaton, fifty-six, Rosbeg, Wesport.)

Beliefs and Customs

Long ago when two parties used to get married, they used to get a fortune of a spinning wheel, a cow, and £20. The parents made the match…

Every aspect of the community's life at the foot of the Reek was governed by traditional observations, and the beliefs and customs that arose from them. They had a strong understanding of the concept of 'Luck'. It was a precious commodity, to be guarded and protected. Luck pertained to all areas of human existence; the house, the cow, making butter, many areas of inter-personal relations, such as meeting strangers, and even observing the moon. People understood that there was a balance, an equilibrium, in all things. That balance was to be maintained at all costs. As well as 'Luck', their superstitious beliefs also dealt with consequences; 'If X happens, then Y will likely follow.' Superstitious beliefs were often juxtaposed with what we might call folk or popular religion. Certain religious customs and emblems, such as Holy water, Brigid's crosses and blessed candles, were credited with special, almost magical, powers. Here we gain privileged inside information on the community's innermost thoughts and fears, the mentality of the time.

In respect of illness, they were just as likely to avail of traditional medicine and cures as orthodox medicine for themselves and their animals. There was a myriad of traditional cures available to them: verbal, manipulative, procedural and herbal. Some were the provenance of certain gifted individuals and others were common knowledge.

Marriage too was surrounded with traditional rites and understandings. It was beginning to change from an economic liaison between families to a romantic relationship between a man and a woman. But matchmaking and the arrangements associated with a dowry were still remembered, and still practised in certain cases. There were lucky and unlucky times to get married and a whole swathe of customs to be observed in relation to the marriage ceremony itself, and the ensuing wedding feast. Some young people were flouting their parents' intentions and arranging 'runaway' matches for themselves, but this was frowned upon.

All year round the calendar was punctuated by festival days, high days and holidays, each having its own customs and rituals. Seventeen festival days are enumerated in chronological order, from St Brigid's day on 1 February, through the year, to the Epiphany on 6 January the next year. The majority have a religious and Christian orientation, many functioning as 'marker' days in the agricultural year. They indicated when crops should be sown and harvested. When a new task was being undertaken, people were observant of the day on which it was begun. Some days were auspicious, good for beginning work. Many festivals such as Hallowe'en and May Day had their roots in pagan antiquity. They were still observed, in a modified form, and keenly anticipated, particularly by the young people. They provided a break from the humdrum of daily life; an opportunity for dressing up, socialising, having fun. They were tied in to the wider culture in a functional way, through the belief system and people's work activities.

We see that time, work and belief were integrated to a remarkable degree, while the traditional understandings still held firm.

SUPERSTITIONS, FOM AND BELIEFS

4.1.1. Superstitious Beliefs (W)

1. Magpies are supposed to be unlucky.
One for sorrow,
Two for joy,
Three for a letter,
Four for a boy,
Five for silver,
Six for gold,
Seven for the tale that never was told.
2. It is unlucky to see a new moon through glass, but lucky to see it when outside. If a person turns three times when he sees the new moon and wishes, he will get his wish before the month is over.
3. When you visit a house it's unlucky not to leave by the same door as you entered, or you will bring the luck of the house away with you.
4. It is lucky to meet a weasel when going on a journey.
5. It is unlucky to meet a red-haired woman first when going on a journey.
6. When you go on a journey don't turn back, it's unlucky.
7. If you visit a house when there is a churning being made, and if you don't help at the churning, there will be no butter on that churning.
8. It's unlucky to throw out water or put out ashes on New Year's Day.

Corpus Christi Procession.

9. It's unlucky to sweep the floor sweepings out the door on a Monday.

10. Never throw out dirty water at night, it's unlucky.

11. You shouldn't use water for the breakfast that's kept in the house overnight, because the fairies drink that water at night. You should always bring in fresh water in the morning.

12. If a cock crows in the door it's a sign of good news.

13. It's unlucky to hear a cock crowing at night. You will hear bad news.

14. If the cock crows three times at night you will hear [of] a death in the family.

15. If you take a lighted coal from the bonfire on Bonfire Night and throw it into the harvest field, there will be a good plentiful harvest.

16. If there is an onion stolen from the vegetable garden, onions won't grow for seven years after.

17. It's unlucky for washed clothes to be stolen from the clothes' line. It is a sure sign of a death in the family.

18. If you wash your face in the dew May morning, you will be an early riser for the year.

19. It's unlucky to have three lights lighting in one room.

20. Never say 'thanks' when you get your fortune told, you break the spell.

21. It's unlucky to visit a new house without bringing a present.

22. If you hear the Banshee crying, you will hear of the death of a friend.

23. It's unlucky to go alone to a wake-house.
24. It's lucky to meet a hare when going on a journey.
25. It's a sign of a death in the family to meet a phantom car.
26. If you lose your way when on a journey at night, take off your coat and wear it again inside out.
27. It's a sign of bad weather to see coloured lights in the fire.
28. To see a straw on a hen's tail is a sign of a funeral.
29. If the hedgehog leaves his nest on Candlemas day, there will be six weeks of bad weather.
30. To dream of chickens is a very lucky dream.
31. If you see a mermaid on a rock and can throw a coat on her, an island will rise up in that place and you will become the owner of it.
32. It's unlucky to walk across a grave.
33. If a coal falls down from the fire, you can expect a visitor to the house.
34. It's unlucky to bring in whitethorn flowers or the foxglove into the house.
(S137: 259–64, Gathered from Margaret Heraty, Carrabawn, Westport.)

4.1.2. *Pisreoga (CBS)*

1. Má fheiceann tú capall bán agus má fhliuchann tú do mhéar le seile do bhéil agus é a chuimilt de do sháil, beidh an t-ádh ort.
2. Má éiríonn tú lá Bealtaine agus d'aghaidh a ní le drúcht, thiocfadh leat éirí i rith na bliana, uair ar bith is mian leat i rith gach oíche, agus deirtear freisin nach bhfaighidh tú bricíní.
3. Má ghlaonn cearc, comhartha báis é.
4. Má thagann tú isteach an príomh-dhoras agus amach an cúl-doras tiocfaidh mí-ádh ar an teach sin.
5. Má tá bó ghá cur agat, tabhair leat giota den seithe nó gheobhaidh ceann eile bás.
6. Má ghabhann easóg romhat ar a'mbóthar tiocfaidh an míthapa ort.
7. Má shiúlann tú trí huaire faoi dhriseach agus tú a'dul ag cearrbhachas, éireoidh leat.
8. Is ceart an bhróg a chur ar a'gcos dheis i dtoiseach.
9. Má leagann tú salann ar a'mbord, fainic nach dtagann an mí-ádh ort.
10. Má bhriseann duine scáthán beidh an mí-ádh air go ceann seacht mbliana.
11. Ní maith an dath é uaithne, ní bhíonn sé ádhmharach.
12. Má fheiceann tú leamhán ag eiteall ar fud an tí, is comhartha é go bhfaighidh tú litir go luath.
13. Má chasann bean mong-ruaidh ar iascaire, fillfidh sé abhaile.
14. Ní ceart a bheith a'breathnú ar ghealach nua tríd an bhfuinneog.

15. Má chuireann tú cuid de do chuid éadaí ort mícheart, beidh an t-ádh ort an lá sin.

16. Ní ceart bualadh amach as teach ina bhfuil siad ag déanamh maistreadh agus do phíopa deargtha agat, gan fód móna a chur ar an tine.

17. Má fhaigheann duine bás i dteach, stop an clog agus díbir an cat amach.

18. Má thiteann gríosach amach as a'tine, comhartha é go bhfuil cuairteoir ag teacht.

19. Má chuireann an cat a dhroim leis an tine, gothadh baistigh é sin.

20. Má fheiceann tú cearc a'fanacht 'muigh faoi mhúr baistigh, comhartha é go bhfanfaidh an lá sin fliuch.

S138: 185-7, Rang 6, Scoil na mBráthar, Cathair na Mart.

Superstitions Translation:

1. If you see a white horse and if you wet your finger with spittle and rub it on your heel, you'll have good luck.

2. If you get up on May morning and wash your face in the dew, you'll be able to get up any time during the night during the next year, and it's also said that you won't get freckles.

3. If a hen crows, that's a sign of a death.

4. If you come in the main door and leave by the back door, bad luck will fall on the house.

5. If you are burying a cow, retain a bit of the hide, or else you'll lose another cow.

6. If a stoat crosses your path, you'll have some mishap.

7. If you walk three times under a briar when you're going to play cards, you'll be lucky.

8. The shoe should be put on the right foot first.

9. If you spill salt on the table, be careful you don't have bad luck.

10. If a person breaks a mirror, he'll have bad luck for seven years.

11. Green is not a good colour, it isn't lucky.

12. If you see a moth flying through the house, that's a sign you'll get a letter.

13. If a fisherman meets a red-haired woman, he'll return home.

14. It isn't right to look at a new moon through the window.

15. If you put on some of your clothes inside out, you'll be lucky that day.

16. It isn't right to leave a house where they're churning, with your pipe lit, without putting a sod of turf on the fire.

17. If someone dies in a house, stop the clock and chase out the cat.

18. If embers fall out of the fire, it's a sign that a visitor is coming.

19. If the cat puts her back to the fire, it's a sign of rain.

20. If you see a hen staying out under a shower of rain, it's a sign that day will remain wet.
(Sixth class, CBS, Westport.)

4.1.3. Emblems and Objects (B'l)

On every St Bridget's Night there is a little cross made by the man of the house. This cross is made of timber and everyone in the house blesses himself with it. Then it is nailed up to the ceiling. It is about four inches in length and two inches in breadth.

Holly with berries is put up at Christmas also, in honour of Our Lord.

On May Eve there are buttercups put on the doors and windows of the house and barns, in honour of the Blessed Virgin.

Palm is worn on every Palm Sunday and then it is put up in the house until Ash Wednesday. Then it is burned into ashes and each member of the house makes a cross on their forehead with it.

Shamrock is worn on St Patrick's Day in honour of St Patrick.

On St Martin's Eve a fowl is killed, generally a goose in honour of St Martin. Some of the blood is spilled outside the door. A cross is also made on each corner of the house and on the middle of the floor.

St Christopher's badge is hung on every motorcar for safety.

When there is a pilgrimage to Croagh Patrick everyone brings a stone and a piece of heather with them in honour of St Patrick.
(S138: 511-12, Obtained by Delia Walsh, Loughloon, from different people.)

MARRIAGE CUSTOMS

4.2.1. Marriage Customs (B'l)

The people of this district usually get married in the period which is called the "seraft". The lucky days for getting married are Wednesday and Sunday. Money and stock are often given as dowry. On the wedding day, when the girl and boy were leaving the house, they used to pelt an old shoe after them. After this the wedding feast is held and the "Strawboys" come, dressed in a way the people will not know them. The captain dances with the bride. They are dressed in their ordinary dress, but they wear a straw hat made by hand. Sometimes the bride would stay in her own house for a month after the wedding. The day that they are coming home from the church they try to avoid meeting neighbours, because they might bring them bad luck. When they were going home they used

Sceach gheal –
whitethorn in bloom.

to go the longest road leading to the house.

(S138: 441, Obtained from John Kearny, sixty-five, and T. O'Malley, sixty-five, Owenwee.)

4.2.2. About Marriage Long Ago (L)

When a young man would be for getting married, himself and his friends would be thinking and guessing where they would get a good girl, that would have money. Then they would pitch on one and the man would send a relative to her house. He would have a pint of whiskey to treat her father and mother and to ask them would they give their daughter to the young man they would mention. Then the father would say he would consider it and they would arrange to meet in town next market day.

On market day all would go to town. The young man would bring his own people and the young woman hers. They would go into a public house and have a few drinks. Here they would make the young people acquainted and then start to make the match. The father would ask the young man how much money he wanted with his daughter; she was a good girl, able to do all kinds of work, and that she was the best girl ever a man reared. Then the young man would say he would want about £80 at least, as he had a good house and land, etc. Then the father would say he would give him £50 and his blessing. The young man's people would speak up and tell him to give some more, that he was a very good worthy young man, etc. Then they would have drinks all round and they would get more fluent in speech. The young woman's father would speak up then and say he would give two calves along with the £50, and that he wouldn't give that to any other man in the parish, but on account of the good character they were, he didn't begrudge it to the young man with his little girl. They all agree to that, have another drink and the match is finished.

Next, they will appoint a day to get married. The father will arrange 'Wednesday' as it is the luckiest day for marriage. They spend the next week making preparations for the wedding. The parties on both sides go about and ask their friends and relations. After that both parties go to town to buy the wedding; they join and purchase all the goods in co. They bring at least 2 barrels of porter, a few bottles of whiskey and plenty of mutton and bacon. Wednesday arrives and all the guests proceed on horseback to the bride's house, every man having his woman behind him on the saddle. They have a good breakfast and some drink and when the appointed hour for the marriage arrives, they all go on horseback and proceed to the chapel. The priest is there, waiting for them. The marriage being over, they all go on horseback again, every man with his woman behind him. They gallop the horses as fast as ever they can till they arrive at the young man's house. All the neighbours cheer and the first man that arrives is the best man. A big dinner is ready for them, and when all have eaten and taken some drinks, night will be drawing on. When night comes on, the dancing begins. Each man, young or old, takes his woman out to dance and when that is over all take a good drink and talk about the times. They sing songs, good old Irish songs, and dance again till they are tired.

The Strawboys come, about 20 of them dressed up in wheat straw around them, and made into hats on their heads. Some of them dress in women's clothing and they dance away for about two hours. The men dividing the drinks go round with a can of porter and give them plenty of it. Another man comes with a bottle of whiskey and when they are satisfied with drink and dance, they bid them goodnight and good luck and go away. The eating and drinking begin again with some good old songs until morning. When morning comes they all get up to go home. They give a hearty shake hands to the young married couple and then go home satisfied after a good night's fun.

[This is written in the exact words used by the storyteller. It was given to me by Kate Sammin who lives in Carramacloughlin.]

In the last ten years or so marriages take place previous to Nuptial Mass in the early morning. The bridal pair go to Dublin, Galway or such like place, on their honeymoon. In some cases they just take a motor drive for the day, returning for the dinner to the bridegroom's house. The old-fashioned weddings are a thing of the past.

(S138: 38-41, An tSr Treasa.)

4.2.3. Local Marriage Customs (Q)

The bride's people invite all their friends to the marriage at the chapel and when it is over they all drive in cars to the bride's new home. That is what is called a 'drag'. They have a great night drinking, singing, and dancing until morning. Matches are often made by the parents of the young couple. In olden times there was no matchmaking. Often a young man would steal a girl out of a window at night, but in these days they will not take a girl unless she has the weight of herself in money.

(S137: 212-3, Kitty Mc Mullin, The Quay, Westport. Obtained from Mrs Derrig, forty-six, The Quay, Westport.)

CURES

4.3.1. Local Cures (T)

It is the general custom when people have certain complaints to use medicine recommended by doctors. But beside those, the old people have cures which when tried prove to be very good.

For instance, a pain in the back can be cured by getting somebody to walk on the back. Food left behind by a ferret is a cure for a sore throat. Sore lips can be cured by making the sign of the cross on each side of the mouth with a coal in a tongs. This is to be done three times on each side of the mouth. Anybody who has never seen his or her father can cure a sore mouth by breathing on it three times. Anybody who takes 'féar gortach' can be cured by eating a bit of grass. The 'féar gortach' is a hunger which comes on a person if he is on a journey.

There is a woman in this district who can take dust out of a person's eye, even though the person might be in another country.

Those are the most important cures known in this district.

(S138: 316, Collected by Nora Flanagan from Mr Anthony Gavin, seventy-six, Scalp, Westport, 18.7.38.)

4.3.2. Local Cures (B'l)

Long ago people used to consult witches for remedies for certain ailments. They could cure a beast from a pain by passing a twine with a knot on it under the beast's belly three times.

Milk left behind by a ferret will cure a cough by drinking it.

People also had certain cures. Timothy Kearns, Owenwee, can cure ringworm. Mrs Grealus, Killeenacoff, can cure a pain in the head, yellow jaundice, the Rose and convulsions by saying certain prayers or other words (unknown). She can also cure haemmorage. Patrick Gibbons, Prospect, has the cure of the latter also. Mrs McEvilly, Letterbrock, can cure the Rose.

Dominick McGreal, Owenwee, can make a cure for sore eyes. Water out of the smith's trough, in which he would be after cooling the red iron, is a cure for sore eyes.

A fox's tongue will draw a thorn out of the body.

The seventh son, if he never saw his father, can cure a sore throat and ringworm.

If you steal a piece of bacon and bury it, it will cure warts.

If you have a sore on your lip and you make the sign of the cross with a gold ring on it, it will cure it.

If you get water in a hole in a rock, people say it will cure warts.

(S138: 449-50, Obtained by Patrick Heraty, Brackloon N. S. from Thomas Joyce, seventy, Owenwee.)

4.3.3. The Cleithín (K)

The cleithín is the spool of a person's breast, fallen down. The way it is lifted is to make an oatmeal cake, the breadth of the mouth of a glass. Leave the cake on the glass and leave the glass on the person's breast. If the spool of the person's breast is down, the cake will stick on to the glass, and keep pulling it up until it has the spool of the breast lifted. Then it is cured. If the spool of the breast is not down, the cake will not stick on to the glass.

(S138: 229, Mrs Gannon, Kilsallagh, 15.3.1938.)

4.3.4. Curing Warts (K)

If a person has a wart on his hand he could get many ways to cure it. If he got ten wisps of straw, put them into a piece of paper and tied them with a string. Leave them on the road, and whoever picks them up would have the warts. There is a little hole in a rock down at Kilsallagh Quay, and if you wash your hand in it the wart would go.

(S138: 231, Margaret Burns, Kilsallagh.)

4.3.5. Boils (K)

To take the top off a boil they used to get a bottle with a wide sgluig (scroig).

They put a little drop of water in the bottle and placed the bottle of water near the fire. When a little steam was seen round the bottle it was placed sgluig downwards on the boil, and it lifted the boil off completely.
(S138: 232, Maggie Gannon, Kilsallagh, 16.3. 1938.)

4.3.6. Local Cures (K)

Garlic is good for a worm in a calf's tail. The people know when there is a worm on a calf's tail, because when they feel the tail the calf looks around. Then they can tell where the worm is. Then they cut the tail where the worm is. They break the garlic with a hammer and mix it with soot. Then they would put it into a cloth and put it around the tail where it was cut. They would leave the cloth around the tail for a week.

The pennywort is good for a pain in a person's ear. It is a round green leaf

Bullaun stone, Aughavale graveyard.

and grows out of the wall. It is heated to the fire until it softens and then left to the person's ear.

An ivy leaf steeped in paraffin oil and rubbed on a corn cures it.
(S138: 256-7, Pat Gannon, Kilsallagh.)

DISEASES IN ANIMALS

4.3.7. *Dry Murrain or Red Water in cattle.*

Red water is taken from a cold in the kidneys and, in nine cases out of ten, it finishes up in dry murrain. The quickest cure for it is a cup of fine salt dissolved in a cup of buttermilk.

Cattle with diarrhoea: boil roots of briars and give them the juice.

Worm in the tail in sheep: split the tail and mix gun powder and garlic and put it in the split.

Buying a horse:

One white foot, buy him.

Two white feet, buy him.

Three white feet, look well about him.

Four white feet, be sure and go without him.

(S138: 168-70, Pupils of Scoil na mBráthar, Rang 6.)

LORE OF CERTAIN DAYS

4.4.1. *Lore of Certain Days (B'l)*

The date, 8 June, of Fr. Manus Sweeny's hanging comes wet every year in West Mayo.

If you be out late on May night, the fairies will bring you and keep you for a year.

If you dirty the water on Whit Sunday you will have no luck; you can't fish or bathe either.

If you wash your head with dew on Good Friday morning, you will never get a pain in your head.

If you cry at New Year's Day you will have sorrow for all that year.

At twelve o'clock on Christmas night all the animals can talk, and the donkey goes down on his knees.

Clew Bay.

A postcard dating from 1939.

Severe Weather.

In the West of Ireland there are many bad storms during the winter. The islands in Blew Bay are a source of shelter, and help to cut away the biggest part of the storm. On November 5th 1926 a big storm arose at about four o'clock in the morning. We were all asleep when Daddy awoke and heard a big crash. He jumped out of bed, and saw the tide rushing into the house. He had just time to call my uncle who came to a back window, and we were handed out to him one by one, rolled up in blankets, as there was no time to dress. One of us was almost forgotten when Mamma heard her saying, "I am here, Daddy." When Daddy ran into her, the bed was floating about the room. The water was five feet high in the house. Everything was destroyed on us, but Daddy and mamma were thankful none of us were drowned. We got shelter in a neighbour's house. We would

not live in our own house for a long time after, as all the floors were lifted, and it was too damp. All the old people say that it was the worst storm for fifty years. Daddy say that when the wind blows from the South West and goes suddenly into the North West. Then the tides rise much higher and may go into the house.

Cissie Hopkins, Rosleg, Westport.
Obtained from
Mrs. Hopkins. Age 45
Rosleg, Westport.

Samples from the original handwritten documents.
Above: 'Severe Weather', as transcribed on p160. *Below*: 'A Game I play indoors', p131.

A Game I play indoor

The game I play is Mrs Browns blackpig. This is the way I play it. First of all you put a lot of children sitting on chairs Then give each child a fortune. Such as a bit of paper, a stick, a bottle, When every child has got a fortune. Go around to each child and ask them a lot of funny questions and if they laugh or answer the question they are out. They have to keep saying Mrs Browns black pig The child that kept up the

best, will kneel down and the child that was asking the questions will stand over the childs head thats kneeling down and say "This is a fortune and a very big fortune and what has the owner of this fortune to do Here are some of the things they have to do One has to bring a can of water, another child has to climb a tree, another child has to wash her face and so on

Jessie Fair Std. 5
Gloshpatrick.

a Game I Play 16 · 5 · 19 38

Skipping.

The game is played in
the following way. A rope is
got sometimes a skipping rope
Two children take a rope each.
A number is said. it might
be a hundred fifty or forty
The competitors start. The rule
is that anyone who stops during
the game is out. Another set
would ~~take~~ take their turn
when the first set finish playing

Sometimes they play
for money. Four players get
a rope each ~~the and~~ start to play.
The one who can play the
longest without stopping is the
winner and he gets the prize.

'A Game I Play: Skipping', p131.

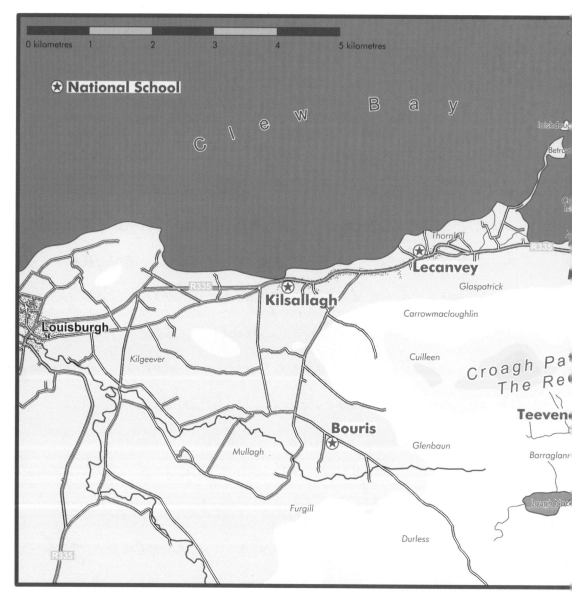

A map of the Westport and Croagh Patrick areas, showing the schools that particiated in the scheme.

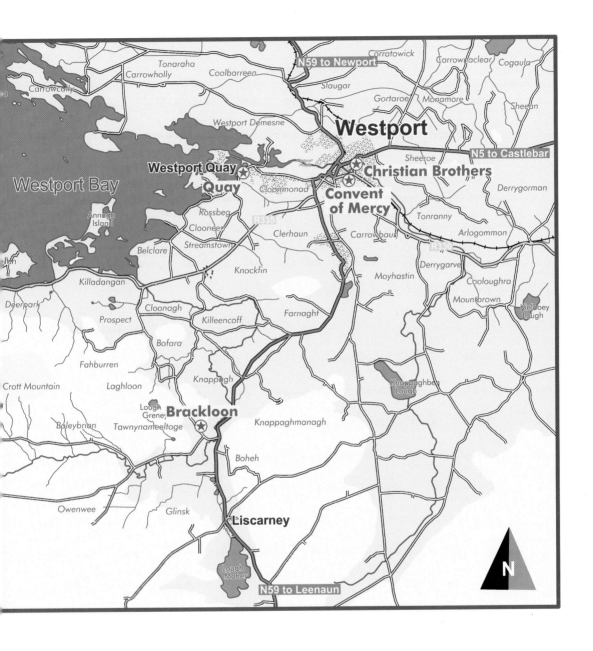

The Local Fairs.

The local fairs were held on the streets in Westport and are still. In some towns they are held on fair-greens. Years ago the buyers came from the country and bought from the men coming in to the fairs. This is not done now. Tolls are paid at about sixpence a head to the Marquiss of Sligo.

When an animal is sold the seller has to give luck-money. If they sell an animal for ten pounds they get five shillings luck-money. When a bargain is made the parties show their agreement by clapping or by spitting on their hands. When an animal is sold it is marked with mud. Sometimes it is marked by cutting a bit of the hair off the side of the animal.

There is a story told of a man who did not sprinkle blood in the four corners of the house on

St. Martin's night. When he was going
to the fair the next morning St. Martin
appeared to him. He asked him why he did
not spill blood in the four corners. The man
said that he had no fowl. St. Martin hit
the cow and she fell. After a while the
road was covered with the blood of the cow.

Dolly Walsh. The Quay, Westport.
Obtained from
Michael Walsh. Age 59
The Quay, Westport.

'The Local Fairs', as decribed by Dolly Walsh, p164.

Maye Joyce shows her son a cart of bonhams at the fair. The last fair was held on 22 May 1976.

A rural scene at the foot of the Reek.

At the same hour on New Year's night the water in the river turns to wine.

If it rains on New Year's night, everyone will have plenty for that year.

(S138:451, Obtained by Sarah Heraty, Brackloon N.S., from John Kearns, Owenwee.)

4.4.2. *The Lore of Certain Days (L)*

The old rhyme about the days of the week is well known in this district:
Monday for health, Tuesday for wealth,
Wednesday the best of all,
Thursday for losses, Friday for crosses,
And Saturday no good at all.
(S138: 51-2, An tSr Treasa.)

4.4.3. *Festival Customs (L)*

Festival days are arranged in order of time, beginning with St Brigid's day.

(i) St Brigid's Day
On St Brigid's day the little girls of the district dress up a doll which they call a 'brídeog'. Then they go from house to house and repeat the following rhyme:

> Here comes poor Brigid both deaf and both blind,
> Put your hand in your pocket and give her a coin,
> If you haven't a penny a halfpenny will do,
> If you haven't a halfpenny God bless you.

The people usually give a few pence. If they ask the children's name it's not customary to tell it.

(ii) St Patrick's Day
The usual Irish custom of wearing the shamrock is carried out on this day. A few of the old men drown the shamrock by taking a few drinks in the public house. There are not any great celebrations to honour the feast but occasionally the Mullagh and Murrisk bands play through the village.

(iii) Shrove Tuesday
Pancakes are made in most homes on this night. The ring is put in the cakes and the old superstition that whoever gets it will marry first is attached to the finding of the ring.

(iv) Ash Wednesday

Crowds attend morning Mass and get the holy ashes. They bring home some of it to those who have not been to Mass. There is a pious belief that the ashes should not be rubbed off on any account until the day is over. Some farmers in this district like to sow their oats on this day.

(v) Holy Thursday

A great number attend Mass and visit the Blessed Sacrament during the day.

(vi) Good Friday

Good Friday is observed something like a holiday. Very little work is done and almost everyone, young and old, go to the church and perform the Stations of the Cross.

(vii) Easter Sunday

There is great rejoicing for the feast. The young children and some of the grown ups too, rise very early to see the sun dancing.

(viii) Whit Sunday and Whit Monday

The people believe that it is not lucky to bathe at Whitsuntide as it is a season of accidents.

(ix) May Day

All crops are supposed to be sown before this date. There is a tradition that no one should touch clay on this day. The children erect an altar in the home, and put fresh flowers on it regularly during the month.

(x) St John's Eve (23 June)

The bonfire is lighted in each village. The children gather turf from village to village. They sit round the big fire and tell stories. A bone is thrown into the middle of the fire. Before they leave some of the ashes is scattered into the fields where the crops are growing.

(xi) 15 August

Many people from this district visit the blessed well in Kilgeever, Louisburgh. Those who suffer from headaches like to make the pilgrimage, they rest their heads on the stone which is supposed to bear the track of the saint's knee. Others make the pilgrimage to Knock.

(xii) 29 September

The first goose is killed for this day's dinner to honour St Michael.

(xiii) Hallow Eve

This is a night of great amusement. The children here look forward to it with great delight. They have barmbrack with the ring for supper. Diving for apples and Snap-Apple are played. The old trick of the three saucers with ring, clay and water is common in the district. Nuts are burned too. When the amusement in the home is over, some of the boys go through the village and throw cabbage stalks at the doors. I don't know what is the origin of this last trick. The púca is supposed to destroy the fruit on this night.

(xiv) Christmas Feasts

There are great preparations for Christmas. The houses are well cleaned; chimneys are swept to give room to Santa Claus. Shortly after nightfall, the big Christmas candle is lighted in the kitchen. Smaller candles are placed in all the other windows, but the people do not leave their big candle lighted all night as they do in other places. The doors are not barred or locked, the belief being that if Our Lord should come, He would find shelter and not be turned away as He was from the doors in Bethlehem. The kitchen and rooms are decorated for the occasion with sprigs of holly and ivy. A motto is hung here and there on the walls, bearing words like, 'God bless our home', 'A happy Christmas', and the like. The children hang up their stockings for Santa Claus.

On Christmas morning crowds attend the early Mass and receive Holy Communion. Greetings of 'A happy Christmas' and 'Many happy returns are heard among old and young. The custom of giving presents prevails in the district. Turkeys and geese are killed for the Christmas dinner. Christmas and New Year cards are sent to friends at home and abroad.

(xv) St Stephen's Day

The boys from each village go, as they express it, 'in the wren'. They dress up in fantastic colours, wearing false beards and carry a box supposed to hold the wren. The children here as a rule do not catch the poor wren, though they carry the box and play a game of pretence. From house to house they travel, standing outside each door, repeating rhymes and playing on a mouth organ. These are the verses used in this locality:

> The wren, the wren, the king of all birds,
> St Stephen's day, she was caught in the furze,
> Up with the kettle and down with the pan,
> Give us some money to bury the wren.

The two last lines are sometimes replaced by these:

> Although she was little, her family was great,
> Stand up landlady and give us a treat.

The boys get a few pence, sometimes sixpence in each house. When evening comes they count the money and divide it equally between them.

(xvi) New Year's Day
The old custom of wishing 'A happy New Year' prevails. Some old superstitions say that if you are sad or joyful this day you will be likewise all the year round. It is regarded as one of the great Christmas feasts.

(xvii) Feast of Epiphany
Commonly called 'Twelfth Night'. Twelve candles – small coloured ones – are lighted in each house. Each member of the family claims a candle in the group. The person whose candle burns out first will, according to tradition, be the first one to die in the family. The Rosary is sometimes recited while the candles are lighting.
(S138: 107-112, This information was supplied by pupils in Stds 5,6 and 7.)

FESTIVAL CUSTOMS

4.5.1. Festival Customs (B'l)
On St Martin's day a fowl is killed and a cross of blood is put on the doors. Sometimes the people make a cross on their forehead with the blood.

On 31 October, which is known as Hallowe'en, there are apples and nuts and there is a feast nearly as good as Christmas. The boys and girls put apples into a tub and go ducking for them, to see who would get the most. Sometimes this night is known as the 'ducking night'.

Long ago some boys were returning home from a dance on November's night. As they were coming along the mountainside they came on a house. They went in and found a lot of fairies dancing. They began to dance also. When they were there a while one said, 'It was time to be going home.' So they all went out but one. The door locked out after them and he could not get out. They told the priest and he said, 'To go there again that night twelve month.' They went there again and found the door open. When they went in, they were all dancing and him in the middle. They told him to be coming home, and he said, 'Cannot ye

wait until I finish my reel?'
(S138: 473-5, Obtained from John and Thomas Joyce, Owenwee, by Patrick Heraty, Owenwee.)

4.5.2. *November's Night (K)*

Long ago the old people used to have a lot of nice customs on November's Night. Some of them are carried on at the present day. They used to steal cabbage, and if they knew of any cross man in the village, they would fling them at his door. Then he would be out after them with his dog. They would fling sticks and stones at him and hunt him into the house. They would have great fun. The boys and the girls used to gather together to a neighbour's house. They used to make a cake and put a ring in it. And whoever would get the ring would be married the first. Then they used to get a tub of water and get an apple and put a half crown into the middle of it and put it into the tub of water, and it would sink to the bottom. Whoever would be the best to get the apple would have it and the money for himself.

They used to leave nuts in the fire and think of names in their minds, and if the nuts would jump, they would be married to the one they named. If the nuts would burn away they would not get married to that one.

They would leave three plates on the table; put soil in one, clean water in the other, and dirty water in the other. Whoever would put his hand into the soil would die before a year. Whoever would put his hand into the dirty water would marry a widow. Whoever would put his hand into the clean water would be the first to go across the sea. They would have a cover on their eyes and they could not see where they would put their hands.
(S138: 247-9, Mr Michael Gannon, Kilsallagh.)

Oral Literature

Once upon a time there lived a family in Carramacloughlin who could not speak any English. Everywhere they went they tried to pick up some of the 'Béarla'. This day three of the lads went to town, listening to everyone they heard speaking English…

People use language creatively, in formal and informal situations. The first story here indicates that language itself has changed in the area in recent times. The language shift from Irish to English had been rapid, without a prolonged bilingual phase. As a result, many of the longer items of oral literature had not passed over into English, though traces of Irish were still to be found in shorter items such as proverbs and riddles.

There are stories about every aspect of life at the foot of the Reek. Stories put a shape on lived experience, make sense of it, process it for the generations to come. They also allow people to dream, to engage in fantasy and escapism. Each story has texture which comes from the way it is fashioned, from the moulding of language, the use of idiom and regional dialect. Storytellers use body language and eye contact, varying their tone for emphasis and atmosphere. Silence and laughter are part of the experience too, though they do not appear in the recorded tale on the printed page.

Local history is preserved in story; stories of St Patrick and the Reek, the Norse Vikings who left buried treasure behind them, supernatural stories about encounters with the fairies and creatures from the spirit world, and the old legends of Fionn Mac Cumhaill and the Fianna. There are folktales too, the oral counterpart of light, popular literature or the DVD. The listeners suspend their disbelief and enter into the conventions of a magical world, where all kinds of exciting events can take place. Many of these stories are local variants of international types which have crossed linguistic and cultural borders easily, because of their timeless and placeless quality.

People's everyday, ordinary, speech is peppered with informal oral literature, in the form of proverbs, riddles and sayings. Proverbs and sayings present a wry, often conservative, look at common problems and happenings in the world. In them, we see people's imaginative use of language. Each proverb they use is a 'speech metaphor' which combines linguistic playfulness with moral training and a philosophical perspective on life. Here is the 'received wisdom' of the community on many issues that affect them. Riddles are mind games which test and sharpen the wits. They are very popular with children, making the child see and understand that all is not as it seems, that there are many ways of perceiving the same thing. The Irish language expression for solving a riddle is, 'Tomhas a fhuascailt', literally 'To liberate a riddle.' The ordinary thing is re-conceived in equally ordinary, but imaginatively extraordinary, terms. Both the hidden objects and the images used to describe them are 'liberated' in being placed side by side in this way.

Life was hard in the 1930s. People used stories to educate themselves, to remember the important events and people, to entertain themselves and sometimes to escape from reality for a while. Their proverbs and sayings have a long-suffering tenor, extolling patience and wisdom in the face of adversity, allowing them to see the world with a wry smile.

HUMOROUS STORIES

5.1.1. Picking up the 'Béarla' (L)

Once upon a time there lived a family in Carramacloughlin who could not speak any English. Everywhere they went they tried to pick up some of the 'Béarla'. This day three of the lads went to town, listening to everyone they heard speaking English. They picked up one word – 'We'. Next day they learned the word 'three'; next day the words 'we met', next day 'by accident'. And lastly the four words, 'he was our enemy'.

On the last day, as they were returning from town, they found a man dead by the roadside. They stood looking at him while meanwhile a policeman came the way. He spoke in English, and they replied, 'We three, we met by accident, he was our enemy.' At once they were arrested and put into prison. When brought before the judge they replied invariably to each question, 'We three, we met by accident, he was our enemy.' For another week they were kept in prison, a puzzle still to the judges.

Finally an Irish speaker was brought along to solve the case, and as he knew both languages the situation was made clear. The prisoners were set free then. (S138: 7-8, Pupil's name: Maggie Gannon, Carramacloughlin. The story was told by Kate Sammin, Carramacloughlin.)

PATRICK

5.2.1. *Cruach Phádraig (B'r)*

Ag an am sin, ní Cruach Phádraig an t-ainm a bhí ar an gcnoc úd, ach Cruachán
Aigle. Agaill an t-ainm a bhí ar an dá bharúntacht seo an uair úd – Agaill na
gCnoc ar an taobh seo den chuan agus Agaill Réidh ar an taobh thoir agus an
taobh thuaidh. Tharla gurb é an cnoc áirithe seo an ceann ab airde ann. Tugadh
Cruachán Aigle air. Is tar éis chuairt Phádraig a hathraíodh an t-ainm go Cruach
Phádraig.

Nuair a bhí an Carghas caite ag Pádraig tháinig deamhain i bhfoirm éanacha
dubha ag cur cathuithe air, ach bhuaigh sé orthu le teann paidreacha. Ar ndóigh
bhí Dia buíoch dhe ansin agus chuir sé aingeal go dtí é lena mhian a thabhairt
dó. Tá sé ráite gurbh é an mhian a d'iarr Pádraig nach gcaillfeadh muintir
na hÉireann an creideamh fíor go deo, agus é féin a bheith ina bhreitheamh
orthu lá an bhreithiúnais mhóir. Deir na seandaoine gur dhíbir Naomh Pádraig
na hollphéisteanna agus na nathracha nimhe as Éirinn an uair seo freisin,
gur chruinnigh sé iad uilig ar bharr na Cruaiche, gur dhíbir sé anuas Log na
nDeamhan iad, gur bháith amuigh sa gcuan iad. Tá barúil (ann) gur thug Naomh
Pádraig cuairt ar Oileán na Cathrach ag béal Chuan Mhódh ar theacht anuas
den Chruaich dó, ach níl aon chruthúnas againn go dtug. Chuir sé teampall ar
bun ag Máigh Umhaill, in aice le Muirrisc, ach ní féidir a bheith cinnte an é sin
an teampall a bhfuil a fhothracha ag Cill a'Ghaobhair nó an ceann a bhí insan
tseanreilig in Achadh Uí Mháille.

D'fhill Naomh Pádraig soir arís an bealach céanna a dtáinig sé anoir trí Achadh
Fhóbhair agus Baile Uí Bhúrca go dtí Baile an Tobair. Ar a bhealach soir dó, chuir
sé mainistir ar bun ag Achadh Fhóbhair, agus cuireadh cloigtheach, nó túr cruinn,
air ina dhiaidh sin, a bhfuil cuid dhe le feiceáil ansin fós. Seanach an t-ainm a
bhí ar an Easpag a chuir Pádraig ar theampall Achaidh Fhóbhair, agus bhí sé ina
fhear chomh humhal, ceansa, cráifeach sin gur thug Pádraig Agnus Dei, nó Uan
Dé, air. Bhí Seanach pósta i dtús a óige agus bhí mac is iníon aige. Aonghus an
t-ainm a bhí ar an mhac agus Mathóna an t-ainm a bhí ar an iníon. Nuair a bhí
Seanach ag tógáil Oird Bheannaithe d'iarr sé dhá impí ar Dhia – nach dtitfeadh
sé féin i bpeaca arís lena bheo, agus fad saoil dá mhac Aonghus. Gheall Pádraig é
sin dó agus bhí a iníon Mathóna ina mnaoi rialta ina dhiaidh sin.
(S138: 202-3, B. Ó Lionáin.)

Translation: *Croagh Patrick (B'r)*

At that time, the mountain wasn't called Cruach Patrick, but Cruachán Aigle.

Croagh Patrick.

Agaill was the name given to these two baronies at that time – Agaill of the Hills on this side of the bay and Level Agaill on the eastern and northern side. As it happened this mountain was the highest of them all. It was called Cruachán Aigle. It was after Patrick's visit that its name was changed to Cruach Phádraig.

When Patrick had completed his Lenten observances, demons came to him in the form of black birds to tempt him, but he overcame them with the strength of his prayers. Of course God was pleased with him then, and He sent an angel to him to grant him his wish. It is said that the wish Patrick asked for was that the Irish people might never lose their faith, and that he himself might be their judge on the Last Day. The old people say that Patrick banished the monsters and snakes out of Ireland at that time also, that he gathered them all on the top of the Reek, till he banished them all down to Log na nDeamhan, and from there drowned them out in the bay. People believe that St Patrick visited Caher Island at the mouth of Clew Bay when he came down from the Reek, but we have no proof of that. He founded a church at Máigh Umhaill beside Murrisk, but we can't be certain whether that is the church whose ruins are at Kilgeever or the one which is in the old graveyard at Aughavale.

Patrick returned the same way he had come, through Aghagower and Ballyburke to Ballintubber. On his way there, he founded a monastery at Aghagower, and a bell tower, or round tower, was put on it afterwards. Some of that can still be seen. The bishop whom Patrick placed in charge of the

Aghagower church was named Seanach. He was such a humble, kind, pious man, that Patrick called him Agnus Dei, or Lamb of God. Seanach had been married in his youth and he had a son and daughter. The son was called Aonghus, and the daughter's name was Mathóna. When Seanach was taking Holy Orders, he asked two requests of God – that he himself might never fall into sin again, and that his son Aonghus might have a long life. God granted those wishes, and Seanach's daughter Mathóna became a nun after that also.

5.2.2. St Patrick (B'l)

Crom Dubh was a man who lived in Liscarney, and he was very rich. When St Patrick was building the tower in Aughagower, this man gave him a bull for food for his men. After this Crom Dubh got sorry for giving the bull. He went to St Patrick and told him to give him back the bull. The bull was killed and St Patrick told his men to gather all the bones and the skin. They did so and St Patrick rose him to life again. Crom Dubh took the bull and went home. It is said that the bull killed him afterwards. After this event the saint went up to the North of Ireland and died and was buried in Downpatrick.

Patrick's Rock in Bohea is called after the saint. There is a blessed well there also. There are a lot of Pats around this district. The 17th of March is celebrated each year in honour of the saint.

(S138: 483-4, Collected by F. Mahon, Brackloon, from Ed O'Malley, about eighty-four, Brackloon.)

5.2.3. St Patrick and the Field in Murrisk (M)

Once upon a time a man came to plough a field in Murrisk. When the horses started to plough the field, the horses would not move a step. The man struck the horses but they would not go. The man sent for the priest. When the priest came he shook holy water on them. The man struck the horses again. The horses galloped through the field. They broke the plough and from that day to this, no one ploughed the field since.

There is a school built in one corner of the field now. There was a black pig seen in the school after it was built. The field is at the foot of Croagh Patrick. It is said St Patrick spent some time praying in this field before he ascended Croagh Patrick.

(S138: 522, Told by John McGreal, farmer, seventy-five, Deerpark, to Martan Mac Gréill.)

5.2.4. St Patrick and the Fallen Angels (M)

Long ago there were a lot of trees growing in this district. There were trees growing up on the hills also. St Patrick used to say Mass on the top of Croagh Patrick. He had a clerk to serve Mass for him.

One day the clerk was out gathering sticks for to light a fire. As he was gathering the sticks he heard a great noise and he looked up. He saw people on every branch of the trees. He was greatly surprised.

All the people spoke to him in one voice and said, 'What will happen to the Fallen Angels on the last day?' They told him to ask St Patrick the next day at the celebration of the Mass.

St Patrick was reading Mass the next day and when he came to the elevation the clerk said to him, 'What will happen to the Fallen Angels on the last day?' St Patrick answered and said, 'Lost, lost, lost'.

When Mass was over St Patrick asked the clerk why did he ask him that question. The clerk said that when he was out gathering sticks the day before, that people came on the branches of all the trees and asked him what would happen to the Fallen Angels on the last day.

St Patrick said the only thing for him to do was to dig a grave for himself. He told him to make the sign of the cross on it with his spade and shovel and then to get into it when the people appeared again. They asked him what did St Patrick say.

The clerk told them what St Patrick said. The clerk then got into the grave and he was just in when all the trees fell. If he wasn't in the grave he would have been killed.

(S138: 531-2, Told by Austin Burke, fisherman, fifty, Murrisk, to Máire Ní Bhrolcháin.)

5.2.5. St Patrick and Ossian (T)

Ossian was one of the Fianna and he had many dealings with St Patrick.

Once when St Patrick was reading Mass, Ossian asked him was there any salvation for the fallen angels but Patrick did not answer until he had finished the Mass.

Then he asked the people who had spoken during Mass and they told him that it was Ossian. Then he went to Ossian and he spoke to him. Ossian told him that a little red man came to him and told him to ask if there was any salvation for the fallen angels. Patrick told Ossian that his days were at an end and he told him to make his grave and to lie within it, and to leave the spade and shovel over him in the shape of a cross. Then the red man came again to Ossian when he was laid in this manner. He would have harmed him but the cross saved him.

Reek Sunday pilgrims on Bridge Street, Westport.

The little red man told him to take the scraw of land and to cut it and that it would make a fire and that was the way that people first found the turf, and he told him other things that were good for Ireland.
(S138: 336, Collected by Nora Flanagan, 22.9.38.)

5.2.6. St Patrick and the Mass Book (T)

There is a story told that one time, as St Patrick left Aughagower to say Mass on Croagh Patrick, he forgot his Mass Book. He did not discern this until he was half way up the mountain. There was such a multitude after him, that when he told them what had happened, the message passed so quickly from one to another that the Book reached the top of the mountain as soon as the Saint.

We celebrate St Patrick's Day on the seventeenth of March. On that day everybody wears a piece of shamrock and the children wear green ribbons. There is a story told of a man who failed to go to Mass on this day and who died suddenly during the day. This is a true story as it happened only fifteen years ago.
(S138: 301-2, Collected by Mary McGreal from Mr Thomas O'Malley, fifty-nine, Owenwee, Westport. 6.5.38.)

5.2.7. *Strange Animals (B'l)*

When St Patrick was praying and fasting on Croagh Patrick, a number of serpents came up out of a place called 'Log na niún' (Log na nDeamhan). These serpents tried to stick their poisoned tongues in this holy man. He fired his Mass bell after them and succeeded in putting them into a lake called Loch na Corra. It is said that a man was looking for sheep and he sat down to rest at this lake. A little woman appeared on a rock, changed into a serpent and dived into the lake. It is said that water horses are still to be found here, and that some have appeared from time to time.

(S138: 514, Collected by Delia Walsh, Loughloon, from Pat Walsh, about fifty-five, Loughloon.)

HIDDEN TREASURES

5.3.1. *Hidden Treasure (L)*

(i) In Clew Bay there is a small island called Inisdaugh. It is the nearest island to the strand at Bartraw. Local tradition claims that it is the richest island in the bay. The story goes that a magic door appears every seven years. This door points to the 'hidden treasure' which is supposed to be a great pile of gold hidden by the Danes. There is a man with a gun across his knees guarding the door. The person who has the courage to enter the cave must shoot this man with a silver coin having a cross on it. This coin is supposed to be a two shilling piece.

___It is told by the natives that a Norwegian sea captain made an attempt to get this hidden treasure. He employed men to dig out to the magic door but his efforts were fruitless, the treasure is still hidden there.

(S138:18 Collected by Willie Fair, Gloshpatrick. Willie got this story from his father.)

(ii) There was a poor scholar going around and he read the lid; no other one could do it. When he was reading it he laughed, and Páidín asked him what was he laughing at. 'It is wrote on this lid,' he said, 'the other side of the tree is a good as this.'

When the scholar went, Páidín went and dug another pot of gold, at the other side of the tree.

(S138: 469-70, Obtained by Delia Walsh from Patrick Gibbons, seventy, Prospect.)

Pilgrims on Croagh Patrick.

5.3.2. Hidden Treasure (Q)

In Clew Bay there are 365 islands – one for every day in the year. The old people say that if you counted the islands in a leap year there would be 366.

One of the islands is called Inisdaugh. There is supposed to be treasure hidden in a cave on this island. It is guarded by a large black rat. It was left there by the Tuatha de Dananns [*sic*]. When they knew that they were getting defeated by the Gaels they cast a magic spell over Inisdaugh. A mist came over it and then the Tuatha de Dananns hid this treasure in it. They left a big fierce rat to guard the treasure and it is supposed to be there guarding it yet. The treasure has never been found.

(S137: 193, Mary Gavin, Knockfin, Westport. Obtained from Eddie Gavin, fifty, Knockfin, Westport.)

5.3.3. The Pot of Gold (L)

Once upon a time there lived in Carramacloughlin a man who dreamt one night that a pot of gold was hidden in Keel Bridge near Ballinrobe. For three nights in succession he dreamt the same dream, so he finally made up his mind to try and secure the great treasure. Off he went, and arrived at the bridge just at midnight. There he met a strange-looking man who asked him what was he looking for. He told the stranger about his dream and was surprised to hear that he – the stranger – dreamt that a pot of gold was hidden in the other man's garden, at home in Carramacloughlin.

Believing the word of the stranger, the first man set off home and began to dig for the gold in the garden. As soon as he started to work, a little man appeared. The little man told him not to touch the treasure as he was guarding it for the fairies. The man went home and told his story. However next day he came again, began to dig and found the gold. He became very rich and lived happily for a long time.

One day a tinker called at this man's house. The woman had a pot on the fire. It was the very same pot which contained the gold. Looking into it, the tinker asked, 'Can you read the story this pot tells you?' The woman only laughed, but the stranger said, 'I'm in earnest; this pot tells there is another crock of gold hidden in your garden. It is on the other side of the bush where you got this pot.' They dug and found the gold. They shared the treasure with the tinker, and all lived very happily and comfortably afterwards.

(S138: 4-5, This story was written by Mollie Gannon, Carramacloughlin. She is in Std 6. The story was told to her by Kate Sammin who lives with the family.)

RELIGIOUS STORIES

5.4.1. The Holy Family (Q)

One day the Holy Family went on a long journey. They sat down to rest under an apple tree. The Blessed Virgin told St Joseph to pick some of the fruit. When St Joseph went to the tree to pick the apples he found that it yielded no fruit. Then the Blessed Virgin heard a voice telling the Child to put His hand on the tree. No sooner was this done than the tree was full of lovely ripe apples. The Blessed Virgin then picked all the apples that she wanted. The apple tree is supposed to be there yet.

When Jesus was on His way to be put to death there were a lot of thorns in his hand. A little robin saw him. He flew down and when he was passing Our Lord he pulled out some of the thorns. This is why all people like the robin. When he was taking away the thorns his breast rubbed against Our Lord's hand. His hand was covered with blood and the blood covered the robin's breast. This is why the robin has a red breast.

(S137: 198-9, Thomas Bourke, The Quay, Westport. Obtained from Mrs Bourke, forty-five, The Quay, Westport.)

5.4.2. *Five Pounds for a Priest's Head (B'l)*

There was a man once and he told his son to go for the priest, that he was ill. When the priest came to hear the man's confession, he jumped out of the bed and cut the priest's head off with a sword. The Government of England was giving five pounds for a priest's head and this man got five pounds for the head.

(S138; 506, Collected by Sarah Heraty, Owenwee, from Peter Gibbons, sixty, Treenlaur.)

5.4.3. *The Friar and His Clerk (T)*

Once upon a time there lived in Killgeever Abbey a Friar and his Clerk. He was very poor and the Christmas was coming, and when Christmas Eve came the Clerk asked the Friar what they would have for their dinner on Christmas Day. The Friar told him to have patience.

It happened that the Friar had a rich brother who lived two miles away. This brother was very rich and he hated the poor people. When Christmas Day came the Clerk said to the Friar, 'It is now Christmas Day and we have still nothing to eat for dinner.' And the Friar said to him that it would not be long now until they should have something to eat. When twelve o'clock came the rich brother had his dinner on the table. All of a sudden the table rose up and floated helter skelter across the fields and hills until it landed at the house of the Friar. The rich man and his servant followed the table but they could not catch up to it until it reached the Friar's house.

When the rich man went into the Friar's house, he accused the Friar of causing the table to come to his house. The Friar did not deny that he caused this happening and the rich man was very angry, but the Friar told him to sit down to dinner with him and to be merry. The rich man did as he was commanded and they feasted royally for that day.

(S138: 307-8, Collected by Austin Flanagan, Scalp, from Mr Anthony Gavin, Scalp, Westport.)

The Fairies

5.5.1. *The Fairies (T)*

The fairies were said to be in Ireland long ago but it is supposed that St Patrick banished them.

It is said that a man and a woman were out one night reaping corn and the bad fairy came to them and asked them if they wanted help. They said they did. Then

Clew Bay.

the fairies began to tie the oats and when they had it tied they stooked it.

Then the fairies asked them if they wanted it threshed and they said they did. They began to thresh the oats on the man and on his wife. The man and woman ran home for safety and closed the door. Some time after, they went to bed and when they got up in the morning not one blade of the oats was cut.

In Drummin a horse was feeding in a field and his tail was platted (plaited) in a way that nobody could loosen it. It was said that it was done by the fairies. (S138: 337, Collected by Nora Flanagan from Patrick Gibbons, seventy-six, Prospect, Westport. 29.9.38.)

5.5.2. *Fairy Abduction (T)*

Nancy Devine was an old maid. She lived with a distant relation of hers in a village not many miles from Croagh Patrick. She made her living by working round the farm and taking care of children for her friend.

In those days the fairies were supposed to visit certain places frequently. There was a place near this woman's home called Carraig na Móna where lights were seen almost every night, and it was believed that this was the meeting place of the fairies. Now Nancy was a brave woman and boasted that she was not afraid to go out alone, night or day. One fine summer evening as she was about to bring home her cows she saw the lights at Carraig na Móna and decided to go and find out for herself if the fairies were really there. When she came within a few yards of the lights she got a great surprise, to see the fairies dancing round a fire in a big circle and seeming to enjoy themselves immensely. Nancy then prepared to go home but she found she was not going to get away from the fairies so easily.

As soon as they laid eyes on her they drew her into the circle, so she had to be content to take her part with the rest of them. Truly she enjoyed the dancing for the first night, but all the time she kept planning how she should get away, for she knew it was not easy to play tricks on the fairies. The dancing continued for three days and three nights and Nancy Devine was getting real tired of her enjoyable companions. She was now determined that she must get the better of them in some way, so she called a halt to the dancing.

She said she wished to treat them for the good time they had shown her in the last three days, but they must allow her to go for some wine and refreshments to celebrate the occasion. The fairies were quite willing to accept Nancy's treat. The chief of the fairies agreed to go with her to get the refreshments, as he did not want her to get away from his notice. She lead him to an outhouse near her home where there was a large bottle of whiskey. This she took back to the other fairies. She treated them all liberally to the whiskey, but was careful to touch none of it herself.

In short, they were all in high spirits with the whiskey and their interest in Nancy began to decline. She took advantage of this immediately and slipped carefully away from her companions.

She was glad to get back home again and tell her friends of her meeting with the fairies. Nancy lived to be one hundred and thirteen years of age, and never forgot her experience with the fairy host.

(S138: 277-9, Collected from Mrs McGreal, forty-five, Scalp, Westport, by Mary McGreal, pupil.)

5.5.3. The Leipreachan (Q)

A man from the Quay caught a leipreachan some time ago. It is said that he found some gold. The leipreachan wears a red suit and a green cap. He is about three feet high. He lives out in the bushes. He mends shoes. He has a pot of gold hidden under the ground. Leipreachans are not looked upon as friendly beings. If anybody has gold and if he buries it down in the ground, the leipreachan will take it and mind it. It is very hard to catch the leipreachan for there are very few in the country.

It is very easy to frighten the leipreachan away. If you wanted to catch the leipreachan you would have to creep up quietly behind him. Then you would

have to keep your eyes on him or he would disappear.
(S137: 209, Mary Ann O'Malley, The Quay. Obtained from Mrs O'Malley, seventy-five, The Quay, Westport.)

5.5.4. Story of a Mermaid (K)

The mermaid appears on a rock before a shipwreck. Jimmy Prendergast saw her sitting on one of the rocks under his own house. She was combing her hair with a comb and a glass. She has a make like a woman. The lower part of her body is fish. She dived into the sea when she saw him and was never seen again.
(S138: 263-4, Mr Michael Gannon, Kilsallagh.)

5.5.5. The Old Hag (Q)

There is an old story told about an old hag that lived in a place called Muine Dearg. This old hag used to change herself into a hare. Every day she milked another person's cows. The man who owned the cows did not know who was milking them. One day he watched the old hag. He had his dogs with him. He caught the old hag milking his cows and he set the dogs after her. The dogs followed her until she went into her own house. The man went into the house but the woman had changed herself into her right form again. The man asked her did she see anything coming into the house. She answered no. The man knew it was the old hag who was milking the cows, as he had heard more stories about her. He told her that if he caught her milking the cows again he would shoot her. From that day out she never went near the cattle.
(S137: 214-15, John O'Malley, The Quay, Westport. Obtained from John O'Malley, fifty-two, The Quay, Westport.)

5.5.6. The Fairy Boat (M)

One night long ago some of the Murrisk fishing boats were out fishing in Clew Bay. The night was very dark. The sea was very rough. Just as they were making for the harbour, they saw a small boat going to an island.

She was so small that the waves used to put her down under the water. The men in the big boats thought it was a boat out line fishing. It was in spring time. She passed the big boats out and when she did, she did not stir, but a small man pulled down sails.

She was not long near the other boats when the small man put a light on her mast, and when the fishermen saw him do this, they knew it was not a real boat. So they started for home.

(S138: 523-4, Told by Patrick Groden, fisherman, forty-five, Murrisk, to Máire Ní Ghrodáin.)

5.5.7. *Fairy Forts (W)*

There is a fairy fort on the Castlebar Road about one mile from the town of Westport. It is a high hill with a mound on the top. People caught a disease called 'Faer Gort' (recte Féar Gortach) there on that spot. A man was found dead near that place and it was said that he died of hunger; that is about twenty-seven years ago. He was found dead standing against a wall and there is a pile of stones there yet and no one ever touched them.

Ten years later a shop-boy was coming from his home to his work in Westport when he was struck with the same disease and he had to get off his bicycle and stand there motionless. A man happened to come along with a cart and the boy asked him to take him in the cart to our house because he was not able to walk. The man lifted him into the cart and brought him to our house. He managed to get as far as the door. My grandmother was in the house and there was a cake at the end of the table and he was not able to ask for a piece of bread because he was speechless, but he took a pinch of cake and ate a bit. He got back his strength. He said that piece of bread saved his life.
(S137: 244-5, Told by Mr John Haran, Castlebar Road, Westport.)

5.5.8. *Fairy Forts (T)*

There are three fairy forts in this district – 'Logan Aifreann' (Log an Aifrinn), 'The Molly', and 'Logan Ore' (Log an Óir). The three of them are in this town land. They are about four miles apart. In shape they are round and are surrounded by stones and blackthorn bushes. In the middle there is a circle of stones and it is supposed to be the hiding place of the Fir Bolgs. There is one fort in the district which is called the 'Molly' and fairies were seen [there] not long ago by the people of the district.

These forts were built by the Danes in olden times and it is supposed that the fairies came to live in them afterwards.

The farmers who own the land where these forts are cannot plough the land or set plants around them, or they are not supposed to take away any of the stones from around the forts. If they do so, bad luck is supposed to fall on them. There was often singing heard in the 'Molly' and music was also heard.
(S138: 332, Collected by Thomas Mc Greal, Tievnacrogha, from Mr James Hastings, seventy-three, Crottmountain, Westport. 29.9.38.)

The Fianna

5.6.1. Fionn Mac Cumhaill (B'l)

One winter's night, as Fionn was sitting in his tent, he heard a whistle coming across the hillside. It seemed to come nearer and nearer every moment. It was not long until he heard the knocking at the door. When he opened it a young girl walked in with a basket in her hand. She left it inside and would not wait to speak. When she went Fionn looked in the basket and found two pups. This is how Fionn got his two famous dogs first.

(S138: 490, Collected by P. Morley from J. Kearns, sixty-five, Brackloon.)

5.6.2. Ossian (T)

After Ossian returned from Tír na nÓg, St Patrick taught him about the true faith.

Now there lived a very old but rich man near Ossian's home. This man owned a very big farm. He had eight sons and three daughters; the sons worked on the farm and the daughters did the housework. If anyone came seeking employment to this man he would put him in prison for three months.

One day as Ossian and four other men were out walking together, the men

Westport Quay and Croagh Patrick.

said to Ossian that they would give him a half gallon of beer to drink if he would go up to the rich man's house and ask for employment. Ossian said he would do that.

He went up to the door and asked for admittance. One of the girls came out to him; he said to her that he wanted employment. She told him the punishment he would get if he told that to her father. Ossian then asked if he could have a talk to her father about it. She then went in to her father and told him that Ossian wanted to talk to him. He came out to Ossian and said in an angry tone, 'Be gone – if you ask employment, or I will put you in prison.' Ossian said he only wanted to be taught the Lord's Prayer. The rich man wondered very much at this, but in order to please Ossian he taught him the Lord's Prayer. He then ordered his daughter to get him a loaf weighing four pounds. He gave the loaf to Ossian along with a shilling and sent him away telling him that if he ever forgot the Lord's Prayer to come to him again and he would teach him.

Ossian went down to the other men fully satisfied. They gladly gave him his reward, being proud of his bravery. From that day forth he was famous as being the bravest man in that district.

(S138: 318-19, Collected by Nora Flanagan, Scalp, from Mr Patrick Gibbons, seventy-one, Prospect, Westport.)

GIANTS AND WITCHES

5.7.1. *Giants and Witches (T)*

At the present day giants are not so common in Ireland as they were in the olden times. There is an account of a giant who could stand on the top of a hill near Croagh Patrick and speak to another giant in the island of Achill, asking him if the potatoes were boiled for his dinner. Then his sight was so strong that when the potatoes were strained he could see the steam rising from them as they lay on the basket. A hop, step and a leap would then land him in Achill. The hop would bring him to Old Head; the step to a rock north of Clare Island and the leap to Achill Head. The potatoes were as big as large turnips and the eyes of them were big enough for the birds to build their nests in them. We do not suppose that such people still exist in any part of Ireland.

There lives a witch in Co. Galway and people go to her for instructions about certain things. For instance, there is a story told about a man in the west of Mayo who built a new house and, when he went to live in it, his sheep and cattle died and the world seemed to go completely against him. A friend of his told him to go to the witch for advice. He did so and she told him to examine the building and to take out any stones on which the mortar or lime did not rest, and to leave them where he had found them. He did so, and from that day forth he prospered. She tells people who lose their butter to go out on May Day and cut an ash plant before sunrise and tie it around the churn to save the butter. There are not many of those witches in Ireland at the present time.

(S138: 326-7, Collected by Marie McGreal, Scalp, from Mr Michael McGreal, fifty-four, Scalp, Westport.)

TALES OF WONDER AND ENCHANTMENT

5.8.1. *Six White Horses (B'l)*

Long ago there were no trees around Brackloon. The people sowed more corn then than they do now. When the corn was ripe in harvest, a good deal of it was often eaten at night and trampled on. For a long time no one knew what was the cause of it. One night a man named Tadhg Rua remained up to watch. It was a moonlight night, and he sat on top of Midgefield Hill, where he could have a good view. After midnight he saw six white horses come out of Loch Gréine and go through all the cornfields. When he told this story, an old man told him to catch one of the horses and keep him in a stable for a year and a day, and he could work him then.

Tadhg succeeded in catching one and he did as the old man told him. After this he took him out, but the horse was still enchanted. He brought the horse to a river to drink and rode on him. The horse ran off with Tadhg on his back, until he came to Loch Gréine. He disappeared under the water with Tadhg on his back. They were never heard of since.

(S138: 492, Collected by P. Morley, Brackloon, from Michael Heraty, fifty, Brackloon.)

5.8.2. *The Gambler (Q)*

Long ago a man whose name is not known now was living at the Quay, Westport. He was always playing cards and he lost a lot of money. He always carried a pack of cards in his pocket.

One Sunday morning as he was going to Mass he met a funny-looking man on the road. The man had a little table and a pack of cards in his hand. He asked the man from the Quay to play a game of cards with him. He agreed, and forgot all about Mass. They began to play and were playing until late in the evening. The man from the Quay was losing all his money. At last he said, 'With the help of

God, I will win this game.' As he said these words the other man disappeared.

He was playing with the devil all the day. From that day onwards he never played cards.

(S137: 194-5, Richard Kelly, Clerhaune, Westport. Obtained from Mrs Kelly, fifty-two, Clerhaune, Westport.)

5.8.3. The Three Requests (W)

There was once a tinker and his name was Tom. He used to go around from house to house mending tin cans and other tin vessels. One day he was crossing a bog and he could not cross it as it was full of bog holes and he said, 'May the Devil take me when I come this way again.'

At last he got out on the road and as he was going along he met a poor woman and she asked him for some charity, and the tinker said that he had three shillings but that he would give her one. And she went her way.

He had not gone far however when he met a poor child, and he gave another shilling to the child. As he went further on he met a poor man who was dressed in rags and he asked the tinker for some charity. Tom told him that he had only one shilling left to get a dinner for his wife and children, but he would give him half of it.

Then the poor man went a short distance away from Tom and shook himself. And all his rags of clothes fell off and he was turned into a beautiful Angel. Then the Angel said to Tom because he was so charitable to the poor to ask three requests and that would be granted to him.

Tom's first request was that his meal bin at home might remain full for a long time. And his second request was: he had a big orchard full of apples, and every year children used to rob it, and his request was that the child who went to take an apple, that his hand might stick to the apple, and the apple to the tree, and remain there till Tom would release it. And his third request was: every time he went to a house, the children of that house were always putting their hands into his budget, and the next time they put heir hands into it, that their hands might remain there till Tom would take them out. Then the Angel granted Tom his requests and went his way.

After a while the meal bin began to get empty and Tom went out begging again. As he was crossing a bog he met the Devil and he said to him, 'Well my man I have you now. For the last time you came this way before you said, "May the Devil take you when you would come that way again." So now you must come along with me.'

'All right', Tom answered. 'I am quite willing. But as we have to pass a village further on, I would not like any of the people to see me walking with you, so you better come into my budget on my back and I will carry you.' 'Right', said the Devil and in he went. But as Tom was passing a forge in the village he stopped, and putting his budget on the anvil, he called to the young boys of the forge to lash the Devil to Hell. And they lashed him, and the Devil was shouting, 'Let me out and I won't trouble you again.' And at last he went away in a ball of fire.

When Tom went home that night he found his wife with a young baby, and Tom went out looking for a godfather for his child. The first person he met was God himself, and He asked Tom what he wanted and Tom told Him that he wanted a godfather for his child. And God asked him would He do. And Tom said 'No', that God was entirely for the rich and not for the poor. And as he was going along he met the Devil, and the Devil asked Tom would he do for a godfather for the child. But Tom said 'No', that he was entirely for the rich and not for the poor. So Tom went his way.

Then Tom met the Angel who first granted him the requests. And the Angel asked Tom what he wanted. And Tom told him he wanted a godfather for his child. And the Angel asked him would he do. And Tom said he would.

When the Angel was leaving Tom, he gave him a little bottle; and he told Tom that any person who was sick to give them a little drop of it and it would cure them.

So Tom went around curing the people and he got very rich. And he went to live in a big castle. One day a widow's son was sick and she sent for Tom. And he came and cured the boy. The widow was very poor and she could not give Tom any money, but she gave him her blessing instead.

Tom was curing everybody and Death was getting nobody. And then it was time for Tom to die, and one day as he was out in his chariot, Death tipped him on his shoulder, and told him to be ready to come along with him. And Tom said, 'All right my man I am ready, but before I go I would like one apple from my old orchard.' And as Death was pulling an apple, his hand stuck to the apple, and the apple to the tree. And he was struggling there, calling to Tom to release him, and he would never bother him again. So Tom released him and he went away.

About a hundred years after, Death visited Tom again. As he was sitting in his castle one night, Death tipped him again, and Tom told him he would be with him when the candle he held in his hand would be burned. And before the candle was burned out, Tom quenched it and buried it. And after a few years Death got it, and burned it, and then it was time for Tom to die, and Death visited him again. Tom said he would be ready to go with Death if he would give him time to say three Hail Marys to make up to God for all the wrong he had done. And Death gave him time. But they were the prayers Tom never said. So Death had to go away again.

One day as Tom was out in his chariot and as they were going over a bridge, Tom heard a cry and he looked down to see a poor soul burning in fire, and the soul told Tom that it was burning there for years for not saying three Hail Marys when it was on earth. So Tom forgot himself and said the three Hail Marys and then Death called him.

Tom was quite willing to go, as he was tired of life. And Death brought him to Heaven, but God would not have him there at all, because he would not let him stand for his child.

Death then brought him to Hell. But the Devil said, 'Take him away for he was the fellow that got me beaten in the forge.' As Tom would not be taken in Heaven or in Hell, Death asked Tom would he like to go back to earth, and Tom said 'No.' He told Death to turn him into a salmon and he went to live in the River Shannon, and he is living there from that day to this.

(S137: 267-75, Written by Mary Geraty. Told by Mrs Lizzie Geraty, Townranny, Westport.)

Ghosts and Spirits

5.9.1. The Ghost in the Graveyard (W)

There was once a crowd of boys gathered together in a drink shop which was situated near a graveyard, and whichever of them would go out to the graveyard and bring in a skull would get a gallon of porter. There was one fellow who said he would bring in the skull. But before he went out, another boy had gone out before him and he had a white sheet around him, and he was standing in the graveyard.

When the boy came out, every skull he would pick up, the person with the sheet would cry out, 'Leave that there, that is the skull of my father.' And so on, he would say it was his mother's and his sister's, and so on.

At last the brave boy picked up a skull and he said, 'Blast you, I'm taking this one, whose ever it is!' So he took the skull and he brought it in, and he got the gallon of porter.

(S137: 276-7, Told by Mrs O'Malley, Ballinrobe Road, Westport.)

5.9.2. The Haunted House (M)

Once upon a time there lived a rich landlord in Murrisk. All the land in Murrisk belonged to him.

There was a certain woman that was not able to pay her rent. She was very poor and she had no way of earning her living. Her only support was a cow and a calf.

When the time came and the woman was compelled to pay her rent, she had to sell her cow and calf in order to pay it. So, she was able to pay the rent this time. But when her turn came again, she had no cow or calf to sell, and she was not able to pay the rent.

When the landlord did not get the rent, he turned the woman out of her house and land. The rich landlord did not live long after that. When he died he could not get into Heaven unless the woman would forgive him for putting her out of her house and land.

Every night they used to hear a noise in the house until the woman forgave the landlord for what he did. The woman who was living there left the haunted house and went to stay in her neighbour's house.

One night a poor old tramp asked her for lodgings for the night. She said she would give him lodgings in a haunted house, and he thanked the woman very much. Just at twelve o'clock he heard great noise in the house. He was a very brave man and he ran to where he thought the noise was. Sure enough, he saw a coffin coming down the stairs, rolling as quick as a flash of lightning. When it had reached the bottom the lid flew off the coffin, and a man walked out of it.

The tramp, not losing his courage yet, asked the man what he wanted, and these are the words the man said, 'I cannot get into Heaven unless the woman forgives me for what I did.' With that, the man vanished.

When morning came the tramp told the woman the whole story. She forgave the landlord and he never haunted her house any more.
(S138: 518-20, Told by Michael John McGreal, farmer, forty-five, to Micheál Mag Réill.)

PROVERBS

5.10.1. Proverbs (B'l)

A stitch in time saves nine.
A bird in the hand is worth two in the bush.
More haste, less speed.
Early to bed, early to rise, makes a man healthy, wealthy, and wise.
To bed with the lamb, and rise with the bird.
A rolling stone gathers no moss.
Never put off until tomorrow what you can do today.
What the púca writes, he can read it himself.

The early bird catches the worm.
New brooms sweep clean.
Too many cooks spoil the broth.
Many hands make light work.
Fine feathers make fine birds.
Empty vessels make most sound.
Time and tide wait for no man.
A watched pot never boils.
A hungry eye sees far.
Waste not golden hours.
Ill got, ill gone.
Ash green is fire for the queen.
It is too late to save when all is spent.
You cannot get blood out of a turnip.
The juice of a cow is good dead or alive.
We never miss the water until the well runs dry.
Every hen should scrape for her own chickens.
Always be honest in thy work and in thy word.
If you do not sow in the Spring, you will not reap in Autumn.
Better late than never.
The help of God is nearer than the door.
You cannot whistle and chew meal.
As long as the fox runs he is caught at last.
Don't judge the book by the cover.
Have yourself or do without.
No use crying over spilled milk.
Spare the rod and spoil the child.
Nearer the church the farther from God.
You cannot put an old head on young shoulders.
There is many a slip between the cup and lip.
The longest way round is the shortest way home.
It is a long road that has no turning.
Courage is half the battle.
Don't count the chickens before they are hatched.
A blind man is a bad judge of colours.
Hunger is good sauce.
A burnt child dreads the fire.
A green Christmas makes a fat graveyard.
What the ear will not hear will not trouble the heart.
A half a loaf is better than no bread.

You cannot have your loaf and eat it.
Beg from a beggar, and you will never be rich.
When wine is in, your wit is out.
A closed mouth catches no flies.
(S138: 468, 470-1, Obtained here and there, Joseph Maher.)

RIDDLES

5.11.1. *A Collection of Riddles (W)*

As I went across the cornfield, I picked up something fit to eat. It was neither fish, flesh nor bone, and I kept it until it ran alone? An egg.

A little round and white house, and it is full of meat, but it has no doors or windows, to let me in to eat? An egg.

Old Mrs Stitcher she has but one eye, and every time she went out a gap she left some of her tail in the trap? A needle and thread.

Which loses the most, a country when it loses its king, or a king when he loses his country? The country loses a sovereign. The king loses only a crown.

What gets wet with drying? A towel.

In comes four legs, picks up one leg. In comes two legs, picks up three legs to throw at four legs, to bring back one leg? A dog comes in and picks up a leg of mutton; a man comes in and picks up a three- legged stool and throws it at the dog to bring back the meat.

What is the best thing out? A house on fire.
(S137: 246-7, Told by Mrs Lizzie Geraty, Townranny, Westport.)

5.11.2. *A Collection of Riddles (K)*

It opens like a barn door, it shuts like a trap, and it's many a thing you will think of before you think of that? An umbrella.

As round as an apple, as deep as a cup, and all the king's horses would not pull it up? A spring well.

Little, little, little, smaller than a mouse; yet it has more windows than in a king's house? A thimble.

As I looked out my window, I saw the dead carrying the living? A boat with men in it.
S138: 251-2, Mrs Gannon, Kilsallagh.

5.11.3. *A Collection of Riddles (L)*

Why is a churn like a caterpillar? Because it makes the butter-fly.

How can you make a slow horse fast? Keep his food from him.

What shows other people what it cannot see itself? A mirror.

If you wanted to light a fire, an oven and the gas, and you had only one match, which would you light first? The match.

Why is a camel a most irascible animal? Because he always has his back up.

Why is a man in front of a crowd well supported? Because he has the press at his back.

Why is a policeman like a rainbow? Because he generally makes his appearance after a storm.

When is a cricketer very cruel? When he bowls his maiden over.

When is a boy in the pantry like a poacher? When he makes for the preserves.

When is a boat in trouble? When it is in straits.

What is the cleanest letter in the alphabet? 'H', because it comes in the middle of washing.

The more you take from it, the bigger it gets… what is it? A hole.

Why is a mouse-trap like a riddle? Because it has a catch in it.

What goes round the world with its mouth open? A beggarman's bag.

Round the house and round the house, and all heads under? The nails in your shoes.

Why does a hen pick a pot? Because she cannot lick it.

Why does a cow look over a wall? Because she cannot look under it.

What is taken from you before you get it? Your photograph.

When is a ship not a ship? When it is ashore.

Flies high, lies low, wears shoes, but has none? A football.

5.11.4. *Riddles (Q)*

How does a sailor know that there is a man in the moon? Because he has been to sea.

How many sticks go to a crow's nest? None, they are all carried.

What is full of holes and holds water? A sponge.

What is the shyest thing in the house? The clock, because it never takes its hands away from its face.

What is always behind time? The back of the clock.

What is the first thing you do when you fall into the sea? Get wet.

Why is a vain young lady like a drunkard? They are both fond of the glass.

(S137: 140-1, Dick Kelly, Clerhaune, Westport. Obtained from Thomas Kelly, fifty-right, Clerhaune, Westport.)

Children's Lore

I often made dolls at home. First I got some coloured cloth and hay. I cut out the shape of the doll's feet, body and head in the cloth. Then I sewed them up and stuffed them with hay…

The children lived in a world before television, videos, CDs, DVDs and computer games. There is a great sense of energy and engagement in their accounts of their games and pastimes. They knew a lot about these topics. They were at pains to give as full a picture as possible of their own particular childhood culture, an area which is often overlooked by adult researchers.

All their traditional rhymes, indoor and outdoor games had been passed down orally, aurally and by imitation. Given the kinds of games they were playing, it comes as a shock to realise that these children were in fact young teenagers (thirteen to fourteen years). The term 'youth culture' had not yet been invented. There is a freshness and innocence about their activities that lets us gauge their mindset. The emphasis is on fun, on structured play as a social activity which binds them together.

Nowhere is their imagination and resourcefulness more evident than when they speak of fashioning homemade toys out of recycled materials such as thread spools and old clothes. The toys gave as much pleasure in their manufacture as in the playing with them. Boys practised for adult activities in hunting and fashioning snares. Girls made rag dolls. A kind of primitive hurling was remembered from a former time, though it seems to have been lost by this stage.

The children obviously enjoyed this opportunity to describe their own activities. With great gusto and confidence, they tell of their own intimate world, where cares seem to have been few and far between.

GAMES

6.1.1. Games I Play (B'l)

Games are played using the following words to select one to hunt the others:
(i) Inkle, ackle, black bottle,
O.U.T. spells out.(Girls)
(ii) Ring a ring o'roses, bottle full of posies,
Ashu, ashu, all fall down.
(Face to the ground – no hunting in this.)
(iii) Sally, Sally Saucer, sitting on a saucer.
Rise up Sally and wipe out your eyes,
Turn to the East and turn to the West,
And turn to the very one that you love best. (Girls)
(Ring of girls, hands joined, going round blindfolded, girl sitting in middle of
ring. When rhyme is finished this girl rises and lays hands on first girl at hand,
who then takes a position in centre, and the game proceeds as before.)
(S138: 458-60, Obtained by Paddy Morley and others from the children.)

6.1.2. Dice (L)

This game is played in the following way. The dice is a small piece of wood with
eight corners, about an inch wide. It is a very suitable game round the fire in the
winter time. There is money left down in playing with the dice. On each side of
the dice there are three, four, five, and six dots. The dots are painted red. In this
piece of wood there is a hole running through the dice and a match through it.
It is played on a level table. Each one takes his or her turn. The first one spins
the dice and it spins a while. At last it topples over and six comes up. They play
on like that until they come to a hundred. The one who gets a hundred first gets
the money at last.
(S138: 62-3, James Fair, Std 5, Gloshpatrick, Westport, 16.5.1938)

6.1.3. The Ghost in the Well (L)

This game is played in the following way.
One boy represents a hen. Three others take the place of chickens. One other
boy takes the place of a ghost. The hen tells one of the hen chickens to go to the
well for water. The chicken goes to the well but the ghost will not let him take
the water. He comes back and tells the hen. Then the hen goes to the well with
her chickens and they see the ghost gathering something. They ask him what

he is doing and he says, 'Gathering stones.' They ask him what does he want the stones for and he says to sharpen his knives to cut the heads off the chickens. He follows them and whoever he catches they are the ghost for the next game. The one he has caught goes into the well, and the other ghost takes his place as a chicken. That's how we play 'Ghost in the Well'.
(S138: 64-5, John Gill, Thornhill, Std 7, Westport.)

6.1.4. Skipping (L)

The game is played in the following way. A rope is got, sometimes a skipping rope. Two children take a rope each. A number is said. It might be a hundred, fifty or forty. The competitors start. The rule is that anyone who stops during the game is out. Another set would take their turn when the first set finish playing.

Sometimes they play for money. Four players get a rope each and start to play. The one who can play the longest without stopping is the winner and he gets the prize.
(S138; 66-7, Tommie Gavin, Std 6, Carramacloughlin, Westport.)

6.1.5. Mrs Brown's Black Pig (L)

The game I play is Mrs Brown's Black Pig. This is the way I play it. First of all you put a lot of children sitting on chairs. Then give each child a fortune, such as a bit of paper, a stick, a bottle. When every child has got a fortune, go around to each child and ask them a lot of funny questions, and if they laugh or answer the questions they are out. They have to keep saying 'Mrs Brown's Black Pig.'

The child that kept up the best will kneel down, and the child that was asking the question will stand over that child's head and say, 'This is a fortune and a very big fortune and what has the owner of this fortune to do?' Here are some of the things they have to do: one has to bring a can of water, another child has to climb a tree, another child has to wash her face, and so on.
(S138: 68-9, Tessie Fair, Std 6, Gloshpatrick, Westport.)

6.1.6. Four Corners (L)

I am going to describe how 'Four Corners' is played.
This is the way we play it. We get four corners. One child stands in each corner. Then one stands in the middle. One runs from one corner to the other corner. The other child runs into the corner the first child has left, and the one in the middle tries to get in the corner too.

Peter Street, Westport.

(S138: 70-1, Julia Agnes O'Malley, Lecanvey, Westport.)

6.1.7. Blind Man's Buff (L)

About four children join in the play. The children make a den first with two chairs. Then they count 'twenty', and whoever twenty falls on must blind. The child that blinds must tie a cloth round his or her eyes so that they can't see anything. The cloth that is round the eyes is called a 'dallóg'. Then the others hide. When the other children have hidden, the one with the cloth round his eyes must look for them. Whoever he catches first must blind again and so on. (S138: 72-3, Sal Gill, Std 5, Thornhill, Westport.)

6.1.8. Colours (L)

This game is played in the following way:
First of all you put the children standing in a line at the wall. Someone is marked out, to give out the colours. Each child gets a colour such as blue, red, white, black, yellow, pink, brown, slate colour, grey, lemon colour, purple, and many others.

There should be a Good Angel and a Bad Angel. The oldest child represents the Good Angel. When the colours are given the Good Angel comes along. The

Sarah Heraty,
Brackloon National School.

one who has given the colours will name them. The Good Angel will pick one. No one is to tell his colour. If the Good Angel picks red, and it's yellow, the one that is giving the colours will tell her to go and learn A.B.C. The Bad Angel comes along. She picks the right one. 'Take her off with you'.

When all are picked, the two Angels catch hands. All the Good Angel has caught line up behind her. All the Bad Angel has caught line up behind her. Each side pulls to see who will win. The Good Angel fails and the Bad Angel wins. Now it is all over at last.

(S138; 74-6, Margaret Gannon, Std 4, Carramacloughlin, Westport.)

6.1.9. Hide and Go Seek (L)

Hide and Go Seek is played in the following way. One of the players says a rhyme:

Hide and go seek, the man is asleep,
The butcher, the baker, the candlestick maker, they all come out of a rotten potato.

Two of the players hide in the den until the others have hidden. One of them goes out looking for the players. When he rises them, they run to the den, trying to get in. The follower sees them coming towards the den. He tries to catch them before they get into the den.

(S138: 77-8, Mick O'Donnell, Gloshpatrick, Westport, 17.5.1938.)

6.1.10. Chip Chop Cherry (L)

The following is the way in which I play Chip Chop Cherry. Two or three children are enough to play it. First they get a pencil and a sheet of paper. Then they draw a round line with the pencil on the paper. Then they take a lot of numbers round the line. When they have all the numbers taken down they have a little rhyme that they say. This is it:

Chip, Chop, Cherry, all the men in Londonderry,
Would not climb up to Chip, Chop, Cherry.

Then they take down the numbers. They finish up then. Then they say it again:

Chip, Chop, Cherry, all the men in Londonderry,
Would not climb up to Chip, Chop, Cherry.

They then keep saying that rhyme until they have the game finished. Then they add all the numbers together, and then they have the game finished. Chip, Chop, Cherry is a very nice game.
(S138: 81-2, Theresa Farrell, Std 5, Lecanvey N.S., Westport.)

6.1.11. Grandmother Grey (L)

Grandmother Grey is played in the following way. The children gather together. They select one who represents the Grandmother. She sits down and the other children repeat this rhyme:

Grandmother Grey, will you let me out to play?
I won't go near the river, or hunt the ducks away.

Then the child who represents the Grandmother says 'No!' The children repeat it over and over until the Grandmother gives her consent. Then the children play about. They pretend they are hunting away the ducks. When the Grandmother sees them she calls them and questions them:

Grandmother: 'Where were you?'
Children: 'Up in Annie's eating bread and jam.'
Grandmother; 'Where is my share?'

Children: 'Up on the loft.'
Grandmother: 'How would I get up?'
Children: 'Sticks and stones.'
Grandmother; 'If I fell down and broke my bones…'
Children: 'Sorra mend you!'

The Grandmother gets up and follows them. The one she catches has to be the Grandmother next time.
(S138: 83-4, Mollie Gannon, Std 6, Lecanvey N.S., Westport.)

6.1.12. Boxes (L)

Boxes are played in the following way. You get a copy [book] and you put a number of dots on it. It is played round the fire in winter time. Two is the number to play.

They get two pencils. Before they start they toss a penny to see who will get the first draw. Whoever will get the toss of the penny will play first. Then they begin to play and they play in turn. You want to be very careful for fear your enemy will get a box.

They play on till the game is finished and then they count the boxes. When you are playing and you get a box you have to put your name in the box. It is a very nice game for the long winter nights.
(S138: 85-6, Willie Fair, Std 5, Gloshpatrick, Westport.)

6.1.13. Cat and Rat (L)

This game is played in the following way. First three children catch their hands together, one in the middle and two each side. One of them stands for the Cat, and another one of them stands for the Rat. The Cat follows the Rat till he is caught. Then the other one is the Cat and he is the Rat. They do the same thing again and again. They keep doing that until they get tired at it. It is a very nice little game for children to play on a fine day outside.
(S138: 87-8, Kathleen Farrell, Std 5, Lecanvey, Westport.)

6.1.14. The Robbers (L)

This game is played as follows. The children stand in a straight line, one behind the other. Each child catches the pinafore or dress of the child before her. Two more catch hands and think of something to ask the children, to take some present, such as a gold palace or a gold castle or anything valuable like that.

Meanwhile the other children who represent robbers recite this rhyme:

How come the robbers, the robbers, the robbers,
And what have you for them?
How come the robbers, the robbers, the robbers,
It's a very fine morning.

They come in under the hands of the other two children. The last robber is caught and asked which would she rather say and take, a doll or teddy bear in gold, or anything else. If they say a doll, they will go on one side. when all the robbers are behind each other they'd draw and whatever side lets out the other side has won.
(S138: 89-91, Margaret Therese O'Malley, Std 7, Lecanvey, Westport.)

6.1.15. Games I Play (T)

In 'Wallflower' the children go around in a ring and repeat the rhyme:

Wallflower, Wallflower, growing up so high,
All those Flowers are all sure to die,
Except this fair maiden, she's the fairest of them all,
She can hop, she can jump,
She can turn her back to the wall.

Then the child whose name is called will turn his or her back to the other children.
(S138: 323-4, Collected by Marie McGreal, Scalp, from Mr Thomas O'Malley, fifty-nine, Owenwee, Westport, 7.11.38.)

Toys

6.2.1. Home-made Toys (L)

(i) Daisy Chains

The girls in this district make daisy chains in summer. They gather a number of daisies, make a hole in the stem of one and pull the stem of a second one out through. This is continued for the length of the chain. Some of the children are good at making daisy chains to decorate a statue of the Blessed Virgin which we have in the school.
(S138: 46, Peggie Lydon.)

(ii) *Homemade Dolls*

I often made dolls at home. First I got some coloured cloth and hay. I cut out the shape of the doll's feet, body and head in the cloth. Then I sewed them up and stuffed them with hay. Next I sewed the feet and arms on to the body. From two round pieces of cloth, I made a head. For the face I sewed on a piece of white cloth, and marked on it, in black pencil, two dots for eyes, a dot for a nose, and a long line for the mouth, slanted strokes over the eyes for eyebrows. Then I dressed the doll with a silk frock made from small pieces. A doll like this is very useful, for when you let her fall she will not break.

(S138: 46, This was written by Peggie Lydon, Thornhill.)

(iii) *How a pop-gun is made*

A piece of stick, generally hazel, or sally, is cut about a foot in length. A hole is bored right through from top to bottom, leaving the outer covering like a shell. A second piece is pared thin enough to go through the first, with a thick portion left at one end, to serve as a handle. A tiny piece of a raw potato is placed on one end of the outer stick and shoved down to the mouth. A second piece of the potato is left at the opening the handle is pushed through. The pressure thus exerted on the air between the two pieces of potato causes the first to shoot out, making the 'pop' noise children love so well. Sometimes they shoot water through the pop gun. This they do by tying a piece of woollen thread on to the handle and soaking it in water. When forcing the air out through the gun the water shoots out with it, a long distance.

(S138: 47, This description was written by John Gill, Std 6, Thornhill.)

(iv) *How a Catapult is made*

To make a catapult you require two strips of rubber, generally parts of an old tyre, a piece of leather (the tongue of an old shoe is most suitable), and a forked branch of a tree.

The rubber bands are about an inch in thickness. They are tied to the top of each branch, and again to the piece of leather in the centre.

To work the catapult, place a stone in the piece of leather. Hold the leather in to your face, then pull the piece of rubber.

(S138: 48, No name given.)

(v) *A Bird Cradle*

These are made from strong and fine sticks and are woven together. The cradle is cone-shaped, with the bottom rod circular in shape and the other in a slanting direction up from it, tapering to a point. Between these thin rods, sally or osier are woven in and out, just like the weaving in a basket. The cradle is used in frosty or snowy weather. It is placed near the dwelling house, convenient to a window. It is raised up a little from the ground by means of a stick to which a long line is attached. Crumbs, meal or such like food are left under the cradle. When the bird comes along he runs in and commences to pick the food. Meantime the boy who sets the trap has the end of the twine farthest from the cradle gripped in his hand. He pulls; the stick comes with him and down falls the cradle, trapping the bird inside.

(S138: 49, Description written by James Fair Std 5, Gloshpatrick, Westport.)

(vi) How to Make a Snare

A snare is made in the following way. Get three strings of snare wire (This is thin wire something like used in bead threading, it is sold for a penny or two pence per roll). Bind the three strings together, plait them, so as to make one fairly strong string. Next cut a number of sticks, short but fairly thick, and fix them into the ground a few feet apart. Tie one end of the snare firmly to the post. Make a loop at the other end about the width of your finger. This helps to catch the rabbit very quickly. The snares must be set low down in the ground. When the rabbit hops along he catches his foot in the loop and is held there. It is necessary to have the little posts fastened firmly in the ground, otherwise the rabbit could easily bring all with him. The constant tugging to try and free himself helps to tighten the wire round the foot.

(S138: 50, This description was written by Willie Fair, Std 5, Gloshpatrick.)

Prayers, Poems and Songs

Mo shlán leat a Mhuirrisc bhreá, shéimhigh, shuairc,
Is do na sléibhte breá meala atá ó dheas is ó thuaidh,
Ba bhinne liom guth crotaigh ag siúl ar do thráigh,
Ná ceolta na cruinne an taobh seo den Chlár.

People often retained the Irish language in the intimate areas of life such as prayers, and sometimes in more structured artistic expression such as poetry and song, after they had ceased using it as the vernacular in every day life. This trend held true at the foot of the Reek also. The folk prayers, poems and songs of the 1930s express religious and emotional truths of the time, in structured, patterned forms. Language here performs an almost ritualistic role – it will not change as fast as in normal speech events. A significant percentage of this material was retained in Irish.

When people said traditional folk prayers they did not talk to God like theologians. They used occasional prayers, which had been transmitted orally, and which were tied to specific contexts. These traditional prayers showed slight textual variation, from person to person and from place to place, because of that oral transmission. Sometimes a prayer was used like a charm, as in the first prayer here which promises eternal salvation for the reciter, if said on nine consecutive Monday mornings. Prayers were used for penitential purposes too. The aithrí (repentance) is said to have been composed by one individual in reparation for his sins and as a warning to others of the consequences of sin. In 1906, Douglas Hyde was very excited to find a version of 'Aithrí Sheáin de Barra' in Mayo. Teacher Breandán Ó Lionáin of Bouris National School gives another version here (7.1.3.), although unfortunately he does not tell us from whom he obtained it. Like Hyde's version, it recounts the nightmare experience of a man sent to Purgatory for three days. There he experienced a vision of the horrors of that place and of the Judgement. He is permitted to return home to warn the living of their potential fate if they do not mend their ways. Such poems excited the emotion of repentance as did prayers like 'Aisling na Maighdine Muire' (7.1.2.), whose recitation, three times before sleeping, was said to ensure eternal salvation for the reciter.

Folk poetry and song provided a kind of metrical and musical chronicle of the important events and people in the locality. A tragic drowning which took place when the ice broke beneath young skaters on Loch Caigain on the Leenane Road, Westport, in December 1896, was recalled in a song (7.2.3.). The community remembered each time the song was sung and listening youngsters learned about the danger of such an activity. A local poet called Robert Cosgrave composed a song about the grain mill that had been turned into a woollen mill in Cloona (7.2.2.). This panegyric song is full of classical references and is poetic local journalism at its best, highlighting the mill's changing role in the local economy.

Over in Murrisk, they still recalled the local song in praise of their own area, 'Slán le Muirrisc' (7.2.1.). Pádraig Ó Loingsigh had collected a version of this song from a Mrs Fitzgerald in Westport in 1802 and Edward Bunting collected the tune from a blind piper and singer named Redmond Staunton. Known also as 'Aoibhneas na gCuan', the version here shows us that the song was still remembered in the 1930s, albeit in a fragmentary form, in the vicinity of Murrisk Abbey where it was first composed.

PRAYERS

7.1.1. Paidir, Márta, 1936 (B'r)

I ngairdín párthais bhí an Páidrín Páirteach
A'moladh na mná bhí ariamh gan locht,
Ó a Rí, is a Rí na nGrásta!
Ná lig fán ar m'anam bocht.
Dhá Rí, trí Rí, braon níor bhlais a mbéal,
Mar tharla Mac Dé go dtug sé an t-uisce tríd a méar.
Is maith an sagart É Mac Dé
Is maith a' baisteadh a rinne Sé,
Nuair bhaist Sé Eoin agus bhaist Eoin É,
Nuair ba mhian le cách a theacht sa láthair
An áit ar crochadh agus ar céasadh É.
Tháinig Aingeal an chreidimh chruaidh
Ar chuairt chuige ar uair a bháis.
Níl aon-dhuine dhéarfas mo phaidir
Naoi n-uaire gach maidin Luain,
Nach dtiubharfaidh naoi naonúr as duais,

Is a anam féin go Flaitheas Dé.
(S138: 207, Fuaireas an phaidir seo ó Bhríghid Bean Uí Ghrádaigh, ninety-six, Coill Saileach Uacht.)

Translation: Prayer, March 1936 (B'r)

In the garden of Paradise, the Rosary was said,
Praising the woman who was ever without fault,
Oh King, and King of grace!
Don't let my poor soul go astray.
Two Kings, three Kings, their mouths never tasted a drop,
As the Son of God came, to take the water through their fingers.
The Son of God is a good priest,
Good is the baptism He made,
When He baptised John, and John baptised Him,
When everyone wished for his coming
There where He was tortured and crucified.
The Angel of the firm faith came
To visit him in the hour of his death.
No one who says my prayer
Nine times every Monday morning,
Will fail to save nine times nine (souls) from trouble,
And his own soul for Heaven.
(This prayer was obtained from Mrs Bridget O'Grady, ninety-six, Kilsallagh Upper.)

7.1.2. Aisling na Maighdine Muire (B'r)

'An codladh dhuit, a Mháthair?'
'Ní hea, a Mhic, acht ag aisling ortsa.'
'Cén aisling í, a Mháthair?'
'Beidh tusa dho do sgiúrsáil, dho do fhóghnáil, dho do splótáil.
Ceanglófar thú de phosta cloiche.
Crochfar thú ar chrann do pháise,
Go dté na táirní maola thrí do chosa is do lámha.
Buaifear cúig mhíle buille ar do chorp naofa,
De na sgiúrsaí luaidh bheas ag dul go cnámh tríot,
Cuirfear coróin spíonta thrí do cheann sáite,
Cuirfear an tsleá nimhe thrí do thaobh deas sáite.'
Íosa: 'Is maith í an t-aisling, a Mháthair.

The Mall, Westport.

An té déarfas an t-aisling trí huaire dul chun codladh na hoíche,
Ní fheicfidh sé damnú síoraí ná pianta Ifrinn choíche.'
(S138: 208, Bairbre Ní Fhlaithbheartaigh, one hundred and two, An Tráigh Bhán.)

Translation: The Virgin Mary's Vision (B'r)

'Are you asleep, Mother?'
'No, my Son, but dreaming of you.'
'What is the dream, Mother?'
'You will be scourged, tortured, flayed.
You'll be tied to a stone post,
You'll be tied to the Passion tree,
Till the blunt nails go through your hands and feet.
Five thousand blows will be rained down on your blessed body,
From the lead scourges that will be going through you, to the bone,
A crown of thorns will be pressed on your head,
The spear of poison will be thrust through your right side.'
Jesus: 'This is a good dream, Mother,
The person who will recite this dream three times when he is going to sleep,
He will never see eternal damnation, or the pains of Hell.'
(Barbara Lafferty, one hundred and two. An Tráigh Bhán.)

7.1.3. *Aithrí Sheáin de Barra (B'r)*

Tá an corp seo sínte go stuama,
Tobac is píopa leagtha ar a uachtar,
Tá na mná óga i ndeoir ar a ngruaidh leo.
Tá na mná aosta 'na suí go stuama,
Tá an t-anam bocht ar thóraíocht an eolais i mbóithrín an chruatain,
Éistidh liomsa agus inseoidh mé scéal díbh,
Cén trí ní tá leis an anam a dhaoradh;
Magúlacht, fáthúlacht, agus bréaga,
Is ó, a Mhuire Bheannaithe, is mallaithe an sgéal é.

I mbóithrín dubh, dorcha, casadh aréir mé,
Bhí sin romham ann – an-spirid na láimhe cléithe,
Bhí cíléar braithlis aige dá fhuaradh
Ag súil le m'anam bocht féin a shloigeadh is a ampladh in éineacht,

Is ann a bhí nidh eile is mó bhí ag déanamh bróin dom,
Mar a bhí, na trí maistíní móra,
An ceann ba lugha, agus ní an ceann ba mhó é,
Bhí a shúil mar an Bhruidhean Caorthainn
Nó coinneal ar thamhnach sléibhe,
Ag súil le m'anam bocht féin a shloigeadh is a alpadh in éineacht.

Is ann a bhí nidh eile is mó a bhí ag déanamh bróin dom,
Mar bhí na trí teinte móra,
An ceann ba lugha, is ní an ceann ba mhó é,
Ba mhó é ná trí mhíle cruach mhóna,
'Gus ná Sliabh Fiollán – cé go mba mhór é.

Is ann a bhí nidh eile is mó a bhí ag déanamh bróin dom,
Mar bhí Iúdás dubh 'na sheasamh romham ann,
Páipéir dhubha aige, agus páipéir bhreaca,
Ceann ina láimh aige agus ceann ar an talamh,
Gach a ndearna mé ó bhí mé 'mo leanbh,
Sgríobhtha síos aige romham go tapaidh,
'Gus ba mhó le m'olc é ná ba mhó le mo mhaith é.

Tháinig sé romham ann, Giúistís na ngúnaí geala,
'Céard a bhí tú a dhéanamh nuair a bhí tú ar an talamh,
Nó an tú an t-anam bocht bhí i gcolainn Sheáin be Barra?'

Ag doras Ifrinn a hordaíodh síos mé,
Deineadh roithleán tollta de mo chroí ann,
Bhí mo chuid feola 'na spólaibh síos liom,
Is mo chuid fola 'rólaibh 'mo thimcheall,
Tháinig Mícheál ArdAingeal romham go héasgaidhe,
Agus bhain sé an bhrí is an gaimh as an méid sin.
Thug sé leis ar an mballa glan, réidh mé.
Ag doras fhlaithis a hordaíodh arís mé,
'Ó, a Mhuire Bheannaithe, sgreadaim ó mo chroí ort,'
Chaith an Mhaighdean Muire í féin ar a dhá ghlúin gheala,
Ghaibh sí cara-is-Críost ag a haon-mhac is ag a leanbh,
'Nár iomchar sé mo laidhbhré ó oíche go maidin,
I ngleann na bpian ná cuir é feasda.
Cuir é ar lúibín claidhe nó fosgaidh,
Nó sa taobh ó thuaidh nuair a shéideas an sneachta,
Nó 'na chasáinín raithnighe ag dul an bealach,
Nó sa gcolainn chéanna arís ar an talamh,
Le teagasc na gCríostaidhe 'gus dá dtabhairt chun aithrighe.'

Níor mhór dom féin go ndearna an congnadh,
Nó san Ifreann íochtarach bheadh m'anam caite,
Sin í anois Aithrí Sheáin de Barra,
Go raibh beannacht Dé ag lucht a héisteachta agus béal a haithrise.
(S138: 209-11, B. Ó Lionáin.)

Translation: The Repentance of Seán de Barra (B'r)

This body is laid out in a sober fashion,
Tobacco and pipe on top of it,
The young women with tears on their cheeks.
The old women are sitting quietly,
The poor soul is seeking knowledge in the ways of hardship,
Listen ye to me and I'll tell ye a story,
Which three things can damn a soul?
Mockery, prophecy, lies,
And oh, Blessed Mary, it's a cursed story.

Last night I happened on a dark, black road,
And there before me – the evil spirit of the left hand,
He had a keeler of spirits cooling,

In the hope of swallowing and devouring my own poor soul.

There was something else there to distress me,
It was, three huge mastiffs,
The smallest of them, and not the biggest,
His eye was like the Bruíon Caorthainn,
Or like a candle in the mountain uplands,
Waiting to swallow and devour my own poor soul.

There was something else there to distress me,
It was, three great fires,
The smallest of them, and not the biggest,
It was bigger than three thousand ricks of turf,
Or Sliabh Folláin – however big that is.

There was something else there to distress me,
Black Judas standing there before me,
He had papers, written and unwritten,
One in his hand and one on the ground,
Everything I had done since I was a child,
He had it written down there in front of me,
And what he had written was a greater cause of harm to me than good.

Then came before me, the Justice of the white robes,
'What were you doing when you were on earth,
Or are you the poor soul who was in the body of Seán de Barra?'
At the door of Hell I was ordered down,
My heart was making a hollow whirring there,
My flesh was hanging down in raw meat,
And my blood coursing around me,
Michael the Archangel came up lightly to me,
And he took the sting and the spite out of all that.
He took me off on the clear, smooth way.
At the door of Heaven I was ordered again,
'Oh blessed Mother, I beseech you from my heart,'
The Virgin Mary threw herself on her two white knees,
She acted as godmother for her only son and child,
'Didn't he wear my livery from night till morning,
In the glen of pain, do not make him go.
Put him in some little nook of a ditch or shelter,

Or up in the North when the snow does blow,
Or as a heathery track going along,
Or in the same body again on earth,
To teach the Christians, and bring them to repentance.'

It must be to myself that help was given,
Or else it's down in the depths of Hell my soul would be cast,
There now is the Repentance of Seán de Barra,
May the blessing of God be on those who hear it, and on those who repeat it.

7.1.4. Prayers (B'l)

When a man is choking we say, 'Deiseal a bhuachaill, (Turn right, boy) pronounced like this, 'Deshill a vochaill'.
When anything sudden happens we say, 'God bless us.'
When a person sneezes we say, 'Dia linn.'
(S138: 509, All the pupils.)

7.1.5. Paidreacha (W)

(i) Cabhair, tarrtháil is grásta ó Dhia dhom,
Agus cabhair gach lá táim 'ga iarraidh Ort,
Sacraimint na haithrí go neartaí Dia sinn,
Coimrigh m'anam ar an Athair Síoraí.
Saol fada agus séan, agus flaitheas Dé go dtuga Dia dúinn ar an lá deiridh.

Translation:

May I have help, redemption and grace from God,
And help every day I ask it of You,
Through the sacrament of repentance may God strengthen us,
May my soul have the protection of the eternal Father.
May we have a long life and happiness, and may God grant us Heaven on the last day.

(ii) Íosa a cheannaigh sinn,
Íosa a bheannaigh sinn.
Íosa a thabharfaidh go Flaitheas sinn.

Translation:

Jesus who redeemed us,
Jesus who blessed us.
Jesus who will bring us to Heaven.

(iii) Mac na hÓighe déan trócaire ar m'anam.
Saol fada le séan, agus Flaitheas Dé go dtuga Dia dúinn.

Translation:

Son of the Virgin, have mercy on my soul.
May God grant us a long life with happiness, and Heaven thereafter.
(S137: 238, D'inis seanbhean ó Dhubhach Beag (Duaig Beag) Maol Raithnigh
an dá phaidir seo don Siúr Bonaventure. *An old woman from Duig Beag, Mulranny,
told these two prayers to Sister Bonaventure.*)

7.1.6. *Píosa cainte a fuaires ó sheanbhean (CBS)*

An t-údar go mbíonn seacht agra ag a mháthair don mhac in aghaidh grá dá
mbíodh ag a mac di.
   Nuair a chuaigh an Mhaighdeán Ghlórmhar go dtí na Flaithis chuir an Mac
fáilte roimpi agus dúirt Sé léi, 'Mo ghrá thú, a Mháthair', agus dúirt a Mháthair
leis, 'Mo sheacht ngrá Thusa, a mhic.'
(S138: 179, C.I. Ó hAoláin.)

Translation:

The reason his mother has seven requests for the son in return for the love he
had for her.
   When the Blessed Virgin went to Heaven, her Son welcomed her and he said,
'I love you, Mother.' And she replied, 'I love you seven times over, my son.'
(Saying I got from an old woman.)

POEMS

7.2.1. *Slán le Muirrisc (B'r)*

Mo shlán leat a Mhuirrisc bhreá, shéimhigh, shuairc,
Is do na sléibhte breá meala atá ó dheas is ó thuaidh,

Ba bhinne liom guth crotaigh ag siúl ar do thráigh,
Ná ceolta na cruinne an taobh seo den Chlár.

Níl na daoine anseo mar chleacht mise, saoithiúil ná suairc,
Acht mar íodhmháigh den ghlas-dair a snuífidhe le tuaigh.
Gheall mé, gan amhras, umhlaíocht don chléir,
Le mo thoil féin a shéanadh ar a dtoil-sean go léir.
Sin é d'fhág mise sa tír seo go buan,
Nó ní thréigfinn choíche Muirrisc, ná aoibhneas na gcuan.

(Sagart d'Ord San Aibhistín a bhí i Mainistir Mhuirrisc agus a athraíodh suas go
dtí Mainistir [blank] a rinne an dán seo, ar fhágáil Mhuirrisc dó. Sagart eile a bhí
insan Mhainistir ar athraíodh an tAthair de Búrca go dtí í a rinne 'An Freagra',
mar fhreagra ar an gceann seo. Is dóigh gurb as an áit sin dó agus an colg atá
air.)

An Freagra
Bíonn fraoich cruaidh casta thiar ar an gCruaich.
Bíonn sioc uirthi, sneachta, gaoth, báisteach is fuacht,
Ní faocháin a chleacht muid-ne, ná báirnigh cladaigh cruaidh,
Acht arán sleamhan cruithneacht', is ní raibh súgh na heorna uainn.
Mura mbeinnse ag géilleadh do Rí na ndual,
Is dá chléir róbheannaithe ag ar fhág sé gach cumhacht,
Ní leigfinnse maslú na tíre ar shiúl
Le haoinne dá maireann, ná leatsa, a Athair Liam de Búrc!
(S138: 212-3, B. Ó Lionáin.)

Translation: Farewell to Murrisk (B'r)

Farewell to you lovely gentle, happy Murrisk,
And to the lovely sweet hills to the north and the south,
Sweeter to me the voice of a curlew walking on your beach,
Than all the music in the world this side of Clare.

The people here are not as I was used to, learned and happy,
But like the branches of the green oak that would be carved with an axe.

I promised, without doubt, obedience to the church,
And to deny my own will above all others,

That's what kept me in this country forever,
And I'd never forsake Murrisk, or the beauty of the harbour.

(It was a priest of the Augustinian Order who was in Murrisk Abbey and who
was transferred up to [blank] Abbey who made this poem, on leaving Murrisk. It
was another priest, who was in the Abbey to which Father Burke was transferred,
who wrote 'The Answer', as an answer to this one. It seems that he was a native
of that place, judging by how angry he seems.)

The Answer

There's tough wiry heather over on the Reek.
And frost, and snow, and wind, and rain, and cold,
It isn't periwinkles we ourselves were used to eating, nor tough limpets,
But fine wheaten bread, and we never wanted for whiskey.
If I hadn't surrendered my will to the King of creation,
And to his blessed church to whom he gave every power,
I wouldn't permit the scorning of this country
By anyone alive, or by you, Father Liam Burke.

7.2.2. Poets (B'l)

Robin [*sic*] Cosgrove lived in Brackloon in a house now occupied by Michael
Heraty. He wrote 'By Brackloon grove I chanced to rove...', and also about the
'Jail'. His father was a poet also but it is not known what he wrote. Robin also
wrote 'Cloona Grand Buildings' (Cloona Mills).
(S138: 456.)

7.2.3. Cloona Grand Buildings – Robert Cosgrove (B'l)

All ye celestial Muses come join me I pray,
In those few lines I'm now going to mention,
It's of a fine prospect that I saw of late,
And to praise it, it is my intention,
That beautiful landscape has dazzled my eyes,
Its beautiful falls put me in great surprise,
And the trees all around it saluting the skies,
For to beautify those grand buildings.

I stood all amazed, on its beauty I gazed,

Murrisk Abbey and Croagh Patrick.

And viewed it with great admiration,
No monarch can boast of so stylish a place,
In any European nation,
St Patrick's mountain alone does preside,
The ships from the ocean sail in with the tide,
And Neptune upon the proud waves he does ride,
With joy at seeing Cloona Grand Buildings.

A beautiful cottage that does it subjoin,
I'm sure adds great fame to its splendour,
All footsteps that pass they give it great praise,
For hospitality and grandeur,
King Solomon's temple I do tell you true,
When on Mt Moriah had no such grand view,
To give it a title, it's right for to do,
I style it the Lodge Mt Moriah.

Early in the morning when the clouds do swell,
If you saw the sun shining on it,
You would think it was Eden's grand gardens to see,

God bestowed such blessings upon it,
The hare and the rabbit are there to be seen,
The snipe and the partridge both flock round the green,
The white trout and salmon in numbers have been,
Come in to see Cloona Grand Buildings.

Nature and art did both take a part,
And bestowed there a liberal bounty,
For the woods and the waters that do it surround,
It's the beauty of all the whole county,
The falls of Niagra were not so complete,
For it manufactures both linen and wheat,
It's fit for the Queen for to wear and to eat,
All dressed by the Cloona Grand Buildings.

All along the banks of the river, throughout the whole spring,
You would hear the nightingale singing,
The lark and the linnet, the blackbird and thrush,
Flock round when they hear the bells ringing;
And the foreign stranger does visit it too,
She comes over seas – now I mention the cuckoo,
She echoes the hills and the valleys all through,
With joy at seeing Cloona Grand Buildings.

And now I do mean for to lay down my pen,
And to say no more of its beauty,
The gentlemen now that possess the place,
To praise them I think it's my duty;
These noble ancestors from Germany came,
They are of the Milesians that first did leave Spain,
Julius Caesar was great, and McDonnell the same,
That now occupy those Grand Buildings.

This song refers to Cloona Mills, Cloona, one mile from this school (Brackloon), where corn, wheat, oats, etc. were ground eighty years ago, and later tweed was woven there from wool got locally. The wool was spun into thread in England, came back to be woven into rough flannel blankets and rugs, shawls, etc. and sent to England once more to be dyed. Then this stuff (some of it) was returned to Cloona for sale, to those who supplied the wool in the first instance, as well as to any other willing to purchase it. J.M.

(S138:498-500, Collected by Thomas F. Maher, from Ed O'Malley, Bofara, Brackloon, Westport.)

SONGS

7.3.1. *Tragic Occurrence at Loch Coggeen, 20 Dec. 1896 (B'l)*

You feeling hearted Christians, I hope you will draw near,
And listen to those sorrowful lines which you shall shortly hear,
Oh it was a sad Christmas for their parents to enjoy,
[blank].

It was at Loch Coggeen not far from Westport Quay,
Where those three heroes lost their lives, I'm sorry for to say.
On the 20th of December, one Sunday afternoon,
How little was their notion they'd meet their death so soon.

They skated round about the lake, as brave as any pair,

Part of the old mill, Cloona.

Till Dudley Toole sprang on the ice, their lives he thought to spare,
They grasped each other tightly, and sank down in the deep,
And closed their eyes to Heaven, for an everlasting sleep.

But when the sad news reached Westport town, at 8 o'clock that night,
They ran in thousands to the lake, to see that awful sight;
To see their aged parents now tearing down their hair,
And they going round Loch Coggeen like people in despair.

Now as they were brought in, and the people standing by,
By that awful sight they got a fright, and surely had to cry,
The other three that then were saved will mind it evermore,
For scarcely they could tell the tale, when they were brought ashore.

Miss Mary-Anne O'Malley, her age but twenty-three,
And Robert McCoy, but twenty-one, a youthful boy was he,
Poor Dudley Toole, scarce seventeen, all in his youth and bloom,
How little did his parents think he'd meet his death so soon.

The day of their sad funeral, it was a mournful sight,
Four and twenty clergy leading, and they all dressed out in white,
The Temperance Band the dead march played, the procession slow moved on,
While the mourners shed a silent tear, their loved ones now were gone.

Now to conclude these sorrowful lines, all you that's standing by,
Implore the Blessed Virgin and her son Who rules on high,
For to give mercy to their souls, let all you Christians pray,
In hope the Lord may pardon them, upon the judgment day.
(S138: 493-4, Collected by P. Morley, Brackloon, from Ed. McManus, sixty to sixty-five, Brackloon.)

7.3.2. The Waters of Clew Bay (M)

Attend your sons and daughters, both husbands too and wives,
On these few lines about Dovins who nearly lost his life,
The cap was blown off his head all on regatta day,
And by the winds was carried to the waters of Clew Bay.

For to regain his head-dress he went to the water's side,
And caught there by the current he was carried by the tide,

The people in breathless haste, spectators stood aghast,
All that day around Clew Bay, thought it would be his last.

There was an eye upon the boy who all thought would be drowned,
It was gallant, brave Mc Auley, the head of Westport town,
To him it wasn't a second thought, he sprang into the bay,
And after the poor drowning boy he nobly swam away.

With boots and clothes you may suppose, it was hard to break the waves,
With courage too, away he flew, young Dovins' life to save,
As soon as he grasped the drowning boy, he held him well afloat,
Until he saw the young lad safe into the arriving boat.

All this time, though wet his clothes, he kept himself afloat,
And would not enter with the boy for to capsize the boat,
This gallant man swam to the land encouraged by the throng,
With might and main, all there in sight, they cheered him loud and long.

So all ye boys of Westport town, I mean big boys and small,
Be careful of the water's edge if you go there at all,
A lesson take of Dovins' case, sure thank God he was safe,
Or else his dear kind relations would surely be bereaved.

It is Head Constable Mc Auley we place him in record,
For his great courageous action we can never reward,
It is a fact around each country town, it is every man's belief,
And soon we will hear in Westport town, he will be made the Chief.
(S138: 533-4, Told by Michael Gavin, sixty-five, fisherman, Murrisk, to Agnes Ní
Ghabhainn.)

Local History

The district was very densely populated before the famine. There were about twice as many dwellings in each village as there are today and there are ruins of houses still to be seen…

The community's sense of place and identity, their understanding of themselves as a people, is expressed in their oral history, or 'seanchas' as it is called in Irish. These stories provide a vital link with the past. They show how the past is remembered in the collective consciousness of the people; which were the important events and who were the important people. Because the process of recalling the past involves forgetting as well as remembering, we can discern which aspects of people's lives were of little consequence, as well as those which were perhaps too painful to be carried along on the river of memory.

Much that was important was never written down. A great deal of the personal, intimate, local details of the community's everyday lives was never formally recorded for posterity. Even if things were written down, it is often only the factual information which is preserved in the record. There may be little or no sense of the emotional aspect of a particular event. In addition, many accounts have been provided by outsiders, be they writers, journalists or government officials. Oral history is a more 'democratic' history. These stories present history 'from the inside out'. They show the process in which the whole community was involved in the weaving of their story up until the present.

The memories range far and wide; from tales of local heroes to accounts of severe storms, accidents and drowning. Each time these stories were recounted the community remembered the chronicle of their past. If the story recalls a tragic event, the listeners may have been reminded about the dangers inherent in their own lives and work.

Surprisingly perhaps, there are few stories about Penal times and the Famine. Such traumatic events are often purposely forgotten by the people who suffered them. If recalled at all, it is in muted tones. The potential feelings surrounding them are so great that the communal memory reacts in a numb, dispassionate way. Accounts of the Famine often intimate that it impacted more greatly in a neighbouring area. Even the memory of it is too hard to bear. But the physical landscape retains the psychic imprint of the tragedies of the Famine in the form of féar gorta(ch) or 'hungry grass'. These are places so marked by the sad events of the Famine that they can still claim a person's life. Standing in such a place causes a debilitating hunger-weakness, which can cause a person to die. People carried oatcake in their pocket while on a journey as a protection against this evil. In 1937 too, people were unwilling to say much about the local landlord and evictions. Michael Davitt's meeting to agitate for land reform had taken place at the Bog Gate on the Newport Road just fifty-five years before, in 1882. This was only yesterday in historical terms.

The humdrum of everyday life was broken by traditional fair days, opportunities for trade and commerce, but also for relaxation and entertainment. Animals were brought into town, tolls were paid to Lord Sligo for permission to transact business on the streets, 'luck-money' was given to complete a transaction. Out in the countryside, a travelling shop brought household requisites which could not be produced at home. Hucksters, peddlers and dealers sold their wares throughout the district. The travelling people, or tinkers as they are properly called, were regular visitors. Their family names were well known. Their visits were welcome, for stories and news and a bit of excitement. But the older custom of settled people gathering around the travellers' fire on their first night in a townland was beginning to give way, to be replaced by a slight sense of alienation and disenchantment. The symbiotic relationship between settled people and tinker, itinerant musician and storyteller was beginning to break down. A new order was coming into being.

Local Heroes

8.1.1. Strong Men (K)

Austin Gill and Patrick Joyce were two noted walkers. Austin Gill walked to Castlebar and back again in two hours and a half. Patrick Joyce, Kinnock, walked to Dublin and back in three days, but he travelled day and night. John O'Donnell from Glosh was a very noted jumper. He jumped five feet eleven at sports in Glosh. Patrick Gill from Westport was competing with him but he could not jump so high. Five feet eleven was the jump. Austin O'Malley, upper Kilsallagh, was a very strong man. He went into Westport with five hundred (weight) of potatoes on his horse. A Civic Guard said he would have him arrested for cruelty to the horse. Austin said what a man can carry, a horse is well able to carry it.
'Let me see you', said the Guard. Austin took it off the horse's back and put it on his own back and carried it as far as the weighing machine.

Patrick Foy, Kilsallagh, was a very noted swimmer. Peter Gill was also a good swimmer. He swam for timber. Patrick Foy was one day out swimming. The tide was just stranding. The other men were outside him. Three big waves rose inside them. Patrick would be dashed against a rock, but for he swam out against a wave. When the other men came in, they did not know what had happened until he told them.

(S138: 265-7, Mr Michael Gill, Kildsallagh.)

ACCIDENTS AND DROWNINGS

8.2.1. The Achill Drowning (L)

Ninety passengers left Achill for Westport on June 4 1893 (recte 1894). They were to take the boat from Westport to Scotland to work in the harvest field. The journey from Achill to Westport was made at that time by boat or on foot. A man named Healy who owned a hooker took the passengers for 6*d* each. They went on board at Darby's Point in Achill.

All went well till they came to Annagh Head near Westport Quay. The Laird steamship S.S. *Elm* that was to take them to Scotland had grounded in the narrow channel off Annagh Head and could not leave until the evening tide. The boatman had to jibe out of the channel to get by the steamer. The captain on the bridge of the steamer called to him to lower his main sail before he would jibe, as the passengers had rushed to see the steamer. He took no notice of the warning but took the swerve and the boat ducked in with all on board.

The officers on the steamer were looking on and immediately lowered lifeboats. They also blew a signal to the Quay and more help was sent out. Fifty-three were picked up; the others, thirty-five in all, were lost. Later their bodies were found and conveyed to Achill in a railway truck. (There was no passenger train to Achill then.) It was the first load of passengers that went by train – mostly dead bodies of young men and women. They were laid to rest in the local churchyard, where lie the victims of the late Kirkintilloch tragedy.

(S138: 23-4, An tSr Treasa.)

8.2.2. A Local Drowning in Clew Bay (L)

The tragedy occurred about the 3rd April 1889. There were three men along with the man who was drowned. Their names were Myles Hynes, Austin Gavin, Pat O'Donnell, and John Hanlon. The latter was drowned.

The accident happened in the following way. They went to the island of Bertraw for four loads of seaweed, or 'wrack' as it is commonly called. The wind

The Town Hall and Clendenning monument, Westport.

was blowing north-west. There was a schooner lying between that island and the island of Inistraugh. They said they would go to see it. They spent a long time examining it. A man who owned the island said if they did not go out at once they would be caught in the tide because it was coming across. The four of them went, filled their loads and began to strike for home. The waves soon rose mountains high. Gavin went first, O'Donnell second and Hynes waited until he had put Hanlon on the horse. Myles Hynes went off then. One wave came and knocked off the load. He was thrown off the horse, the load along with him. Another wave came and swept one cleeve off. He clung to the cleeve (it was cleeves all four had) on the west side. He never got the other one from that forth. Just then the horse gave a plunge and swept him about ten yards. He was safe at that moment. Looking back he saw Hanlon behind, a few feet from a channel. His load had fallen too. He had a cap belonging to Hynes. He waved his hand just as he was going across the channel. A wave came and broke the hangings of the cleeves. Down went horse and man.

The police and people were looking for him all through the strand, thinking that he would be brought ashore. But they were disappointed. They were sent out the next day with boats to look for him. A lot of boats passed beside him. The steersman saw his hand about an inch down under the water. He caught hold of it and dragged him to the shore. He was brought to his own house where an inquest was held. He was found on the opposite side of the island where he was

drowned. They found the horse afterwards. This boy was about 30 years of age.
(S138: 24-6, Written by Thomas Gavin, Carramacloughlin, Westport. The story was
told by Thomas Walsh, Carramacloughlin, grandfather of the boy who wrote it.)

SEVERE WEATHER

8.3.1. *The Big Wind (L)*

The Big Wind was in the year 1839. In the evening the sky got very red and it
began to blow. In a short time the wind increased to a terrible gale and a fierce
storm blew. It knocked the stacks of oats and ricks of hay. The storm grew
stronger and stronger until it brought the roofs off some of the thatched houses
and one could see the sheaves of oats flying by in the air. The people were
terrified. In Killsallagh, about 2 miles from Lecanvey, there were 32 houses, but
they were all knocked except 12 on that awful night.
(S138: 29, This short account was given by Kate Sammin, Carramacloughlin.)

8.3.2. *A Terrific Storm (T)*

On the evening of the second of December, 1927 there were a number of
fishermen out in their boats off the west coast of Mayo. They had been fishing
for a good while, when, about eight o'clock, a great storm arose. Their boats
were not able to withstand the tempest, and after the fierce struggle with the
wind, twenty men were swept away. The storm began to abate about twelve
o'clock and much harm had been done during the terrific gale.

At daybreak their families were expecting the men home, but, as they were
not coming, they began to get alarmed and a party immediately went in search
of them. After a few days the bodies were washed ashore at different places along
the shore. There were ten of them buried on the little island of Iniskea. It was a
very sad sight to see, ten men being buried together in one grave. All the families
were grief stricken when they heard of the disaster. It also caused great anxiety
throughout Mayo.

There were many trees blown down and some cattle killed that night. There was
a motorcar proceeding from Westport to Drummin and it was swept off the road at
Knappagh and blown into the bogs. The people who were in the car were thrown
out and received minor injuries. It was a night to be remembered by the people of
this district for many years and everybody was glad when calmness came.
(S138: 280-1, Collected by Mary McGreal, Scalp from Mr Edward O'Malley,
Owenwee, Westport, 11.11.37.)

The Quay, Westport.

8. 3.3. Severe Weather (Q)

In the West of Ireland there are many bad storms during the winter. The islands in Clew Bay are a source of shelter, and help to cut away the biggest part of the storm. On 5 November 1926 a big storm arose at about four o'clock in the morning. We were all asleep when Daddy awoke and heard a big crash. He jumped out of bed and saw the tide rushing into the house. He had just time to call my uncle who came to a back window, and we were handed out to him one by one, rolled up in blankets, as there was no time to dress. One of us was almost forgotten when Mamma heard her saying, 'I am here Daddy.' When Daddy ran into her, the bed was floating about the room. The water was five feet high in the house. Everything was destroyed on us, but Daddy and Mamma were thankful none of us were drowned. We got shelter in a neighbour's house. We could not live in our own house for a long time after, as all the floors were lifted and it was too damp. All the old people say it was the worst storm for fifty years. Daddy says that when the wind blows from the southwest and goes suddenly into the northwest, then the tides rise much higher and may go into the house.

(S137: 196-7, Ceura Hopkins, Rosbeg, Westport. Obtained from Mrs Hopkins, forty-five, Rosbeg, Westport.)

Train at Westport Quay.

PENAL TIMES

8.4.1. Penal Times (B'l)

There is a Mass Rock in Bohea, about half a mile south east of the school. It is situated near a graveyard which is known as Cillín. It is said that St Patrick said Mass there on his way to Croagh Patrick. There is a Blessed well and the relics of an old church to be seen there yet. There is a Mass Rock in Boleybrian at the south side of the Reek, about a mile west of this school.

There is another one in Prospect.

(S138:442, Obtained from Thomas Joyce, Owenwee, and Pat Gibbons, Prospect.)

8.4.2. In the Penal Times (L)

There is a field in Gloshpatrick called Log an Aifrinn. An old woman named Mrs Fair, who died last year (1937), at the age of 84, told that she heard from her parents that Mass was said in this valley.

(S138: 41, An tSr Treasa.)

The Famine

8.5.1. *Famine Times (B'l)*

The Great Famine did not affect this district very much. It was not thickly populated. There were a few houses then occupied but are now in ruins. The blight fell on the potato crop, and they all failed, and rotted afterwards in the pits. The people had to live on cabbage, turnips and other vegetables, and also frogs, snails, cattle and seaweed.

(S138: 457, S. Ó Meachair.)

8.5.2. *Féar Gortach Stone (K)*

The féar gortach stone is a stone on the left hand side of the road beyond Kilsallagh School. There is a track of a crow's foot on the stone and the old people tell us that if a person sat on it they would get féar gortach. It is also called cloch a scarta because the old people used to get scraith cloch on it and they used to dye their clothes with it. But all the people in this district call it the féar gortach stone.

(S138: 230-1, Margaret Burns, Kilsallagh, 15.3.1938.)

8.5.3. *Stories of the Famine (K)*

In the year of 1846 a terrible famine swept all over the country. Heavy blight fell on the crops and destroyed them. No person could get food and most of them died from hunger. Whatever place they happened to die they would be buried in that spot. They used to put marks with a stone over the grave so that they would know where they would be buried.

Near Mr Gavin's house in Kinnock there is a grave. There is another in Austin Grady's field. On top of the bray (brae?) of Boreen Johnston a lot of people were buried. They died on their way going to Leenane for food. They were all buried in that place together.

(S138: 262, Mr Michael Gannon, Kilsallagh.)

The Landlord

8.6.1. *The Landlord (B'l)*

Lord Sligo is the local landlord of this district. The family has been settled here

Bridge Street, Westport.

for about a hundred years. He was looked upon as a good Lord. People were evicted when they would not pay their rent. Long ago, people could not cut turf or sticks on their land without acquainting the landlord.
(S138: 486, Collected by P. Morley from T. Joyce, seventy, Brackloon.)

8.6.2. Land League Meeting (CBS)
At the Bog gate off the Newport Road in 1882 Parnell, Davitt and Dillon were present. Parnell counselled the people to hold on to their farms.
(S138: 173, C.I. Ó hAoláin.)

FAIRS, BUYING AND SELLING

8.7.1. The Local Fairs (T)
The fairs of this district are held in Westport, Murrisk, Drummin and Aughagower. Cattle are bought and sold at Westport, Drummin and Aughagower and sheep at Murrisk. Sometimes people transact business at the farm houses. There are certain streets set apart for the fair in Westport. The cattle and sheep are on the streets [set aside] for themselves, and the horses on

Fair day on the Fair Green, Westport.

a square for themselves.

At the entrance to the fair there is a customs, and anybody who has bought cattle or stock of any kind has to pay some money coming out from the fair. When people sell stock they pay what is called luck-money. This luck-money is calculated according to the price of the animal. When a bargain is made, the parties concerned strike hands to show that they are satisfied.

When animals are sold, they are marked with mud or paint to separate them from other animals. It is also the custom in such cases to keep the halter rope which binds it (the animal) beforehand.

(S138: 305-6, Collected by Mary McGreal from Mr Dominick McGreal, fifty-two, Scalp, Westport. 19.5.38.)

8.7.2. The Local Fairs (Q)

When an animal is sold, the seller has to give luck-money. If they sell an animal for ten pounds, they get five shillings luck-money. When a bargain is made the parties show their agreement by clapping or by spitting on their hands. When an animal is sold it is marked with mud. Sometimes, it is marked by cutting a bit of hair off the side of the animal.

There is a story told of a man who did not sprinkle blood in the four corners of the house on St Martin's night. When he was going to the fair the next morning, St Martin appeared to him. He asked him why he did not spill blood in the four corners. The man said that he had no fowl. St Martin hit the cow and she fell. After a while the road was covered with the blood of the cow. (S137: 182-3, Dolly Walsh, The Quay, Westport. Obtained from Michael Walsh, fifty-nine, The Quay, Westport.)

8.7.3. Buying and Selling (L)

Shops were not as common in the olden days as they are now. Travelling people used to sell goods to dwellers in the district. An old man from Aughagower used to go from house to house selling tea, sugar, candles and other household requisites. He had a horse and kind of covered cart, in which he carried his goods. Buying and selling were not carried on after Mass.

Sometimes work was done for the shopkeeper in exchange for goods. The words 'boot', 'tick' and 'change' were, and are, used, still. 'Boot' refers to part

In the Demesne.   *Westport, Co. Mayo.*

In the grounds of Westport House.

payment for goods, 'tick' when no money is given but time is allowed to pay, 'change' – the money returned after paying full price. Friday is regarded as a lucky day to buy or sell. Markets were held in the neighbouring towns, where they are still held.

Hucksters, peddlers and dealers travel yet through the district with their wares. They buy feathers and rags. The ordinary names are given to the coins. Sometimes a £5 note is called a fiver.

(S138: 132, Written by Johnnie Gill, Thornhill, Std 7. The information was got from his father and old men in the district.)

SPORTS

8.8.1. Hurling and Footbal (B'l)

Long ago the people used to go hurling with rough hurleys and a wooden ball. The wooden ball was made from a thread spool. The matches were played between every two townlands. They were always played in a field. They were generally rough and had hardly any rules.

(S138: 488, S. Ó Meachair.)

TRAVELLERS

8.9.1. Travelling Folk (B'l)

Travelling people visit this district occasionally. They have been coming for many years, and they are very poor. Some of them sell small articles to the people. They sleep in a certain house in every village. They get food from the people, and they give them alms of bottles, wool, irons and rags, which they sell. They travel by foot, and sometimes horse and trap. Sometimes they travel singly, and other times families go about. Sarah Fallen, John Reilly, Con Hegarty, are the best known in this place. The Wards, Maughans, Collins, and Mongans are the most that visit this district. The day before, or after, a fair day, they mostly come. Some of them can tell your fortune by looking at your hand or by cutting the cards. The first night after they come, the people gather around them to hear stories of other places. The most of these have canvas covers for over them at night, and they camp beside a wood where they will have shelter and timber to make a fire. Now and again, Kelly the hawker from Westport, comes round selling cloth and clothes of all kinds.

Tinkers' tent.

Sarah Fallen takes nothing but wool and is fed and kept in any house she arrives at in late evening, 'Sleáimín o'Wool' (nickname). The Maughans, Wards, Mongans, Collins are the usual tinker class. Their women beg, the men buy and swop inferior animals and can 'make money'.

(S138: 452-3, Obtained by Sarah Heraty, Brackloon N.S., from John Joyce, seventy-five, Owenwee.)

8.9.2. Travelling Folk (L)

Travelling people still call at houses in the district. They have been doing so for a number of years. They are usually very poor.

Such people sell articles like needles, pins, glasses, combs, hair slides, paper flowers. The tinsmiths, or tinkers as we call them, sell cans and saucers. These they make themselves. They make the flowers also, but the other articles they get in large shops in the towns, for a few pence. Sometimes the rich people give them small articles free.

They camp on lonely roadsides or mountain paths; occasionally they sleep in disused barns or old houses. They generally travel in bands. They have a few carts and quite a number of donkeys, with an occasional old thin horse. They get their food from the people, accepting whatever is offered them. The people give them potatoes, flour, milk, bread, vegetables, and perhaps a few pence.

The best known in this district are Mahons, Collins, Wards, Mongans, Barretts. They come for the fairs in Westport and Louisburgh, also for the pattern in Murrisk which takes place on the last Monday in August.

Nowadays they do not tell stories. Neither do the local people gather round them for news.

(S138: 52-3, An tSr Treasa.)

Afterword

I am not a native of Westport. We came to live in the town thirteen years ago and like many of the other 'blow-ins' here, we have found it a most congenial place to live. There is a strong sense of community, strong enough to welcome the stranger and their contribution also. Working with the material from the Schools' Collection has given me a great sense of the place, of the richness of its living cultural heritage over time. The beautifully handwritten accounts by the children of the late 1930s take one right into the heart of the community at that time, in a way few other historical resources could. It has been a deeply enriching experience.

When all the material from the nine schools was transcribed initially, it came to some 80,000 words. This publication only allowed for a little over half of that material to be included. The selection of texts for inclusion was extremely difficult. These texts are chosen just as a representative sample of the whole. But I content myself with the knowledge that all the transcribed material will be preserved and made accessible when it is presented to Mayo County Library, where it can be consulted.

It is sometimes difficult to believe that only seventy years have elapsed since these accounts were collected. So much has changed in the intervening years. The value of the Schools' Collection is increasing for us today, filling in a part of our story in this place which might otherwise be forgotten in the hustle and bustle of modern living.

As I worked with the material, in all its diversity, I often felt it could be likened to a blueprint for living, a template for survival in the townlands at the foot of Croagh Patrick. We are grateful for the energy and the dedication of the teachers and pupils who saved it for us. It is a fitting and moving tribute to their memory.

Glossary of Irish Words and Phrases in the English Texts

Airgead lóchra (luachra): meadow sweet (2.10.3.)

Báiníns: jackets (2.12.1.)

Bean Shee (bean sí): fairy woman (3.4.1.)

Béarla: English (5.1.1.)

Botháin: huts (2.1.2.)

Botharlán (buachallán): ragwort (3.3.2.)

Brídeog: homemade effigy of St Brigid (4.4.3.)

Cailleach: 'hag', bed in outshot beside the kitchen fire (2.1.1.)

Cailleach dhubh: cormorant (3.4.2.)

Caisín: upper part of the churn (2.5.1.)

Carraig na Móna: rock of the turf (5.5.2.)

Carraigín Dilisc: little rock covered in dulse (3.5.2.)

Cipín: small stick (3.1.2.)

Claibín: wooden bowl with a hole in it (2.5.1.)

Cleithín: ensiform cartilage (4.3.3.)

Clúbhán: ? (3.3.2.)

Créachtar (créachtach): loosestrife, crane's bill (3.3.2.)

Féar gortach: hungry grass (4.3.1.)

Fearbán: buttercup (3.3.1.)

Fóidín: green scraw/sod (3.2.1.)

Gad: withe (2.5.1.)

Go mbeirimid beo ag an am seo arís!: May we be alive and well a year from now! (3.2.1.)

Gríosach: hot embers and ashes (2.4.2.)

Hugaibh! Hugaibh! (chugaibh): To you! Mind out! (2.14.1.)

Láighe: loy, spade (2.7.1.)

Liaghán: part of potato left when 'slit' is cut (3.2.1.)

Log Aifreann (Log an Aifrinn): Mass Hollow (5.5.8.)

Logan Ore (Log an Óir): Hollow of gold (5.5.8.)

Losset (losaid): dough tray (2.4.3.)
Noggins (naigín): small wooden cup (2.2.1.)
Púca: pooka, fairy sprite (5.10.1.)
Riabhóg: pipit (3.4.2.)
Scraith chloch: rock lichen (2.6.2.)
Scraith fhliuch: seaweed (2.10.1.)
Sgluig (scroig): neck of a bottle (4.3.5.)
Troighthíní: stockings without soles (2.14.3.)
Tuighe-bualach(buarach): rope made out of rushes (2.6.2.)
Woreach (bórach?): crooked, mis-shapen feet (2.14.3.)

Image Acknowledgements

I would like to express my sincere thanks to the individuals and institutions who were so helpful in my search for images for inclusion in *Ag Bun na Cruaiche*.

Aiden Clarke photographed images on pages 20-24, 27, 41-51, 68, 95, 114, and 152.

Aiden also obtained image on page 63 from the family of the late Jim Lavelle, R.I.P.

The images on pages 39, 57, 67, 87, 106, 109, 118, 132, 142, 158, 160, 161 and 163 are reproduced from the Harry Hughes's Collection of postcards, with kind permission.

The image on page 26 is reproduced from the memorial booklet *St Columbkille's National School (The Quay School), 1886-1986*, Westport, 1986.

The images on pages 25, 29, 30, 34 and 133 are reproduced from *Schooldays in the Shadow of Croagh Patrick*, Westport, 1999, by kind permission of Caitríona Bn. Uí Raghallaigh.

Liamy McNally kindly provided the images on pages 31 and 164.

Críostóir MacCárthaigh, Lárionad Uí Dhuilearga, Ollscoil na hÉireann Baile Átha Cliath provided the images on pages 77, 111, and 167, which are reproduced with kind permission.

The images on pages 15, 17, 80. 82, 83, 150 and 165 come from the postcard collection in Mayo County Library's Local Studies' archive.

The images on pages 73 and 91 were taken by the author.

COLOUR SECTION

Clew Bay, courtesy of Aiden Clarke.

Postcard from 1939, and the rural scene at the foot of the Reek, courtesy of Mayo County Library Local Studies' Archive.

Map of the Westport and Croagh Patrick areas, courtesy of Barry Dalby of EastWest Mapping.

Maye Joyce and son, courtesy of Liamy McNally.